A Baker's Dozen
Easy Crochet
DOILIES ™

Contents

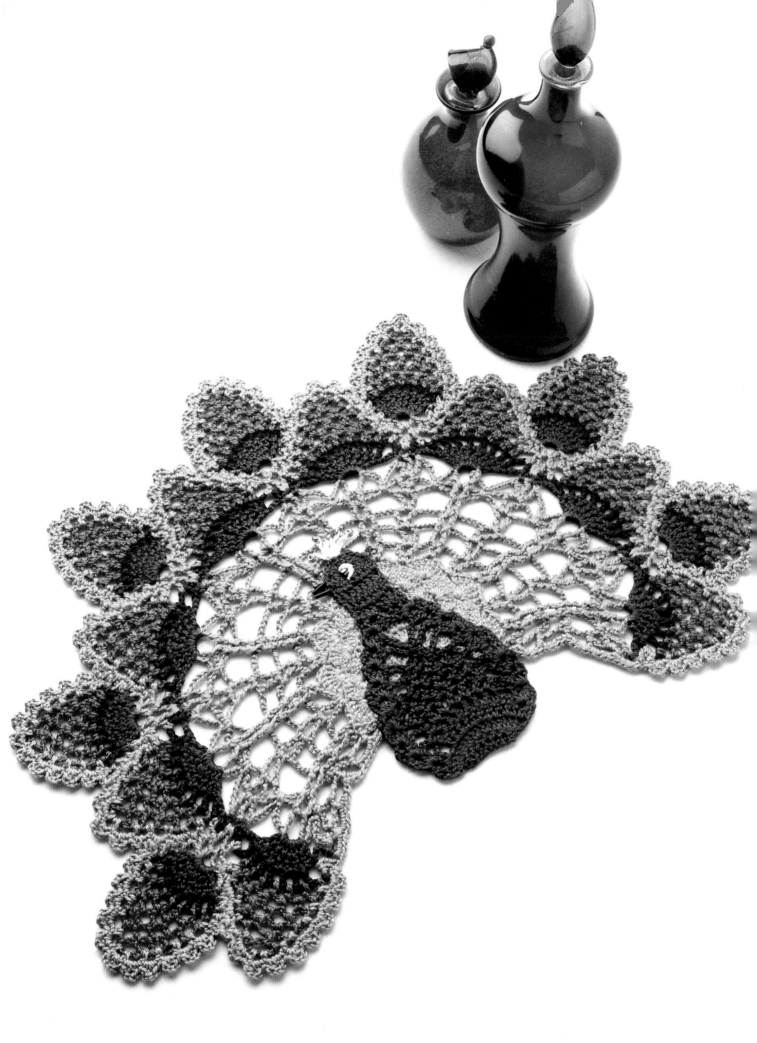

Peacock
Doily

DESIGN BY **LISA OBERDORF**

SKILL LEVEL

EASY

FINISHED MEASUREMENTS
9½ x 12½ inches

MATERIALS
- DMC Pearl Cotton size 5 crochet cotton (27 yds per skein):
  3 skeins #988 medium forest green
  2 skeins each #309 dark rose and #796 dark royal blue
  1 skein each #977 light golden brown and #823 dark navy blue
- DMC Cebelia size 30 crochet cotton (567 yds per skein):
  2 yds #B5200 white
- Sizes 10/1.15mm and 6/1.80mm steel crochet hooks or size needed to obtain gauge
- Embroidery needle
- Sewing needle and thread
- 3mm blue beads: 5
- 3mm black bead
- ¼-inch-long black tubular beads: 2

GAUGE
Size 6 hook: 5 dc = ½ inch; 5 dc rows = ½ inch; 7 pineapple rows = 1¾ inches

PATTERN NOTES
Weave in loose ends as work progresses.

Join with slip stitch as indicated unless otherwise stated.

Chain-3 at beginning of row counts as first double crochet unless otherwise stated.

Chain-6 at beginning of row counts as first treble crochet, chain 2 unless otherwise stated.

SPECIAL STITCHES
Scallop: (Sc, dc, ch 2, dc, sc) in same st.

Beginning shell (beg shell): (Ch 3, dc, ch 2, 2 dc) in same st or sp.

Shell: (2 dc, ch 2, 2 dc) in same st or sp.

3-double crochet cluster (3-dc cl): [Yo, insert hook in indicated st, yo, draw up a lp, yo, draw through 2 lps on hook] 3 times, yo, draw through all 4 lps on hook.

DOILY
TAIL
Row 1 (RS): With size 6 hook and light golden brown, ch 8, **join** (see Pattern Notes) in first ch to form a ring, **ch 3** (see Pattern Notes), 11 dc in ring, turn. (*12 dc*)

Row 2: Ch 3, dc in same dc as beg ch-3, 2 dc in each rem dc across, turn. (*24 dc*)

Row 3: Ch 3, dc in same dc as beg ch-3, dc in each of next 4 dc, 2 dc in next dc, dc in each of next 3 dc, 2 dc in next dc, dc in next dc, 2 dc in each of next 2 dc, dc in next dc, 2 dc in next dc, dc in each of next 3 dc, 2 dc in next dc, dc in each of next 4 dc, 2 dc in next dc, turn. (*32 dc*)

Row 4: Ch 1, sc in each of next 15 dc, 2 sc in next dc, sc in each of next 16 dc, turn. (*33 sc*)

Row 5: Ch 1, sc in first sc, [sk next sc, 5 dc in next sc, sk next sc, sc in next sc] across, turn. (*8 5-dc groups*)

Row 6: Ch 3, 3 dc in first sc, sc in 3rd dc of next 5-dc group, [7 dc in next sc, sc in 3rd dc of next 5-dc group] across, ending with 4 dc in last sc, turn. (*7 7-dc groups, 2 4-dc groups*)

Row 7 (RS): Ch 1, sc in first dc, 7 tr in next sc, [sc in 4th dc of next 7-dc group, 7 tr in next sc] across, ending with sc in last dc, **change color** (see Stitch Guide) to medium forest green. Fasten off light golden brown.

Row 8: Ch 6 (see Pattern Notes), tr in same st, [ch 4, 2 dc in 4th tr of next 7-tr group, ch 4, (tr, ch 2, tr) in next sc] across, ending with ch 4, 2 dc in 4th tr of next 7-tr group, ch 4, (tr, ch 2, tr) in last sc, turn.

Row 9: Sl st in first ch sp, ch 6, tr in same sp, [ch 5, **fptr** (see Stitch Guide) around each of next 2 dc, ch 5, (tr, ch 2, tr) in next ch-2 sp] across, turn.

Row 10: Sl st in ch sp, ch 6, tr in same sp, [ch 5, **bptr** (see Stitch Guide) around each of next 2 tr, ch 5, (tr, ch 2, tr) in next ch-2 sp] across, turn.

Row 11: Sl st in ch sp, ch 6, tr in same sp, [ch 7, fptr around each of next 2 tr, ch 7, (tr, ch 2, tr) in next ch-2 sp] across, turn.

Row 12: Sl st in ch sp, ch 6, tr in same sp, [ch 8, bptr around each of next 2 tr, ch 8, (tr, ch 2, tr) in next ch-2 sp] across, turn.

Row 13: Sl st in first ch sp, ch 6, tr in same sp, [ch 5, sc over ch sps of rows 11 and 12 tog, ch 5, fptr around next tr, ch 3, fptr around next tr, ch 5, sc over ch sp of rows 11 and 12 tog, ch 5, (tr, ch 2) twice and tr in next ch sp] across, ending with ch 5, fptr around next tr, ch 3, fptr around next tr, ch 5, sc over ch sp of rows 11 and 12 tog, ch 5, (tr, ch 2, tr) in last ch sp, turn. Fasten off.

Row 14: Join dark royal blue in first ch sp, ch 1, sc in same ch sp, *ch 4, tr in next ch-3 sp, (ch 1, tr) 7 times in same ch-3 sp, ch 4, sk next ch-5 sp, sc in next ch-2 sp**, ch 3, sc in next ch-2 sp, rep from * across, ending last rep at **, turn. Fasten off.

Row 15: Sk first sc and next ch-4 sp, join dark navy blue in first tr, ch 5 (counts as first dc, ch 2), dc in next tr, [ch 2, dc in next tr] 6 times, *ch 4, sc in next sc, ch 3, sc in next sc, ch 4, dc in first tr of 8-tr group, [ch 2, dc in next tr] 7 times, rep from * across, leaving last ch-4 sp and last sc unworked, turn. Fasten off.

FIRST PINEAPPLE
Row 16: Join dark rose with sc in first ch-2 sp of row 15, [ch 4, sc in next ch-2 sp] 5 times, ch 2, dc in next ch-2 sp, leaving rem sts unworked, turn. (6 ch-4 sps)

Row 17: [Ch 4, sc in next ch-4 sp] 4 times, ch 2, dc in next ch-4 sp, turn. (5 ch-4 sps)

Row 18: [Ch 4, sc in next ch-4 sp] 3 times, ch 2, dc in next ch-4 sp, turn. (4 ch-4 sps)

Row 19: [Ch 4, sc in next ch-4 sp] twice, ch 2, dc in next ch-4 sp, turn. (3 ch-4 sps)

Row 20: Ch 4, sc in next ch-4 sp, ch 2, dc in next ch-4 sp, turn. (2 ch-4 sps)

Row 21: Ch 4, sc in next ch-4 sp, turn. Fasten off.

2ND–7TH PINEAPPLES
Row 16: With finished Pineapple to the right, sk next ch-4 sp, sk next ch-3 sp and next ch-4 sp of row 15, **join** dark rose with sc in first ch-2 sp of Pineapple on row 15, [ch 4, sc in next ch-2 sp] 5 times, ch 2, dc in next ch-2 sp, leaving rem sts unworked, turn. (6 ch-4 sps)

Rows 17–21: Rep rows 17–21 of First Pineapple.

EDGING
Row 22 (RS): Join medium forest green at base of first st on row 8, [4 sc along end of next row] 6 times, work (tr, dc, sc) along end of row 15, *ch 3, sc in first ch sp of Pineapple, [ch 3, sc in next ch sp] 4 times, ch 3, (sc, ch 3, sc) in sp at tip of Pineapple, [ch 3, sc in next ch sp] 5 times**, ch 3, dc in ch-4 sp of row 15, (dc, ch 3, dc) over ch-3 sps of both rows 14 and 15 tog, dc in ch-4 sp on row 15, rep from * across, ending last rep at **, ch 3, (sc, dc, tr) over end of row 15, [4 sc along end of next row] 6 times, sl st in base of last st on row 8. Fasten off.

Row 23: Join medium forest green to tr before First Pineapple, **scallop** (see Special Stitches) in each of next 11 ch-3 sps, *sc in next ch-3 sp, dc in next ch-3 sp, (dc, ch 3, dc) in next ch-3 sp, dc in next ch-3 sp, sc in next ch-3 sp, scallop in each of next 9 ch-3 sps, rep from * 7 times, work scallop in rem 2 ch-3 sps, sl st in next tr. Fasten off.

PINEAPPLE 2ND ROW
Row 1: Join dark royal blue in ch-2 sp of scallop just before ch-3 sp between Pineapples, tr in ch-3 sp, (ch 1, tr in same ch-3 sp) 7 times, sl st in next ch-2 sp of next scallop, turn. Fasten off.

Row 2: Join dark navy blue in ch-2 sp of scallop just above where dark royal blue is joined, dc in first tr, [ch 2, dc in next tr] 7 times, sl st in ch-2 sp of next scallop, turn. Fasten off.

Row 3: Join dark rose with sc in first ch-1 sp, [ch 4, sc in next ch-2 sp] 5 times, ch 2, dc in next ch-2 sp, turn. *(6 ch-4 sps)*

Rows 4–8: Rep rows 17–21 of First Pineapple.

[Rep rows 1–8 of Pineapple 2nd Row consecutively] 6 times.

EDGING
Row 9: Join medium forest green to ch-2 sp of 9th scallop, ch 1, sc in same sp, dc in ch-2 sp of next scallop, sc in first ch sp of Pineapple, [ch 3, sc in next ch sp] 5 times, ch 3, sc in same ch sp as last sc, [ch 3, sc in next ch sp] 5 times, dc in next ch-2 sp, sc in ch-2 sp of next scallop, turn.

Row 10: Work scallop in each ch-3 sp, sl st to first sc of previous row, turn. Fasten off.

For row 9 of next Pineapple, sk next 3 scallops on row 23, then join medium forest green in ch-2 sp of next scallop.

Rep rows 1–10 for rem 6 Pineapples.

BODY
Row 1: With size 6 hook and dark royal blue, ch 10, dc in 3rd ch from hook, dc in each rem ch across, turn. *(9 dc)*

Row 2: Ch 3, dc in same st as beg ch-3, 2 dc in each dc across, turn. *(18 dc)*

Row 3: Ch 3, dc in next dc, ch 2, 2 dc in next dc, ch 3, sk next 2 dc, dc in next dc, [ch 1, dc in next dc] 7 times, ch 3, sk next 2 dc, 2 dc in next dc, ch 2, dc in each of next 2 dc, turn.

Row 4: Sl st into ch-2 sp, **beg shell** *(see Special Stitches)* in same ch-2 sp, ch 3, sk next ch-3 sp, dc in first dc of 8-dc group, [ch 2, dc in next dc] 7 times, ch 3, **shell** *(see Special Stitches)* in next ch-2 sp, turn.

Row 5: Sl st into ch-2 sp of shell, beg shell in same ch-2 sp, ch 4, sk next ch-3 sp, sc in next ch-2 sp, [ch 4, sc in next ch-2 sp] 6 times, ch 4, shell in ch-2 sp of shell, turn.

Row 6: Sl st in ch-2 sp of shell, beg shell in same ch-2 sp of shell, ch 4, sk next ch-4 sp, sc in next ch-4 sp, [ch 4, sc in next ch-4 sp] 5 times, ch 4, shell in ch-2 sp of shell, turn.

Row 7: Sl st in ch-2 sp of shell, beg shell in same ch-2 sp, ch 4, sk next ch-4 sp, sc in next ch-4 sp, [ch 4, sc in next ch-4 sp] 4 times, ch 4, shell in ch-2 sp of shell, turn.

Row 8: Sl st in next ch-2 sp, beg shell in same ch-2 sp, ch 4, sk next ch-4 sp, sc in next ch-4 sp, [ch 4, sc in next ch-4 sp] 3 times, ch 4, shell in ch-2 sp of shell, turn.

Row 9: Sl st in next ch-2 sp, beg shell in same ch-2 sp, ch 4, sk next ch-4 sp, sc in next ch-4 sp, [ch 4, sc in next ch-4 sp] twice, ch 4, shell in ch-2 sp of shell, turn.

Row 10: Sl st in next ch-2 sp, beg shell in same ch-2 sp, ch 4, sk next ch-4 sp, sc in next ch-4 sp, ch 4, sc in next ch-4 sp, ch 4, shell in ch-2 sp of shell, turn.

Row 11: Sl st in next ch-2 sp, beg shell in same ch-2 sp, ch 5, sk next ch-4 sp, sc in next ch-4 sp, ch 5, shell in ch-2 sp of shell, turn.

Row 12: Sl st in next ch-2 sp, beg shell in same ch-2 sp, ch 5, sk next ch-5 sp, sc in next sc, ch 5, shell in ch-2 sp of next shell, turn.

Row 13: Sl st in ch-2 sp of shell, beg shell in same ch-2 sp, shell in ch-2 sp of next shell, turn.

Row 14: Ch 3, dc in next dc, [2 dc in next ch-2 sp] twice, dc in each of next 2 dc, turn. *(8 dc)*

Rows 15 & 16: Ch 3, dc in each dc across, turn.

Row 17: Ch 3, dc in same st as beg ch-3, dc in each of next 6 dc, 2 dc in last dc, turn. *(10 dc)*

Row 18: Ch 3, **3-dc cl** *(see Special Stitches)* in next 3 dc, dc in each of next 2 dc, 3-dc cl in next 3 dc, dc in last dc, turn. *(6 sts)*

Continued on page 37

Birds of a Feather
Doily

DESIGN BY **LINDA DEAN**

SKILL LEVEL

EASY

FINISHED MEASUREMENTS
9½ inches wide x 33½ inches long

MATERIALS
- Universal Yarn Nazli Gelin Garden 10 size 10 crochet cotton (308 yds per ball):
  1 ball #700-36 barn red
- Size C/2/2.75mm crochet hook or size needed to obtain gauge
- Tapestry needle

0
LACE

GAUGE
5 sps = 2 inches; 12 dc = 2 inches; 6 rows = 2 inches

PATTERN NOTES
Weave in loose ends as work progresses.

Chart-reading knowledge is necessary.

SPECIAL STITCHES
Space (sp): Ch 2, sk next 2 dc or sk next ch-2 sp, dc in next dc.

Block: Dc in each of next 3 sts or 2 dc in next ch-2 sp.

Beg block increase (beg block inc): Ch 5, dc in 4th ch from hook, dc in next ch, dc in next dc.

End block increase (end block inc): *Yo, insert hook in base of last dc made, yo, draw up lp, yo, draw through first lp on hook, [yo, draw through 2 lps on hook] twice, rep from * twice.

Continued on page 37

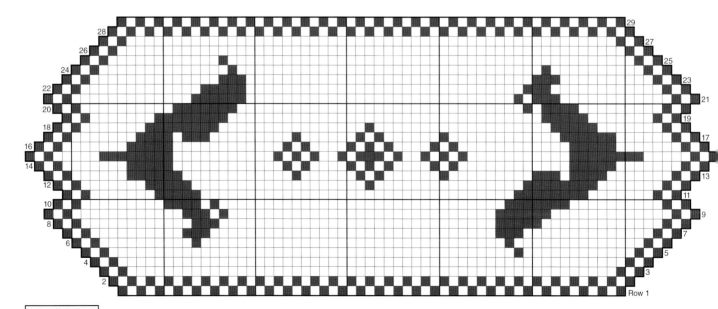

Birds of a Feather
Chart
Note: End block inc and beg block inc are explained in Special Stitches within pattern.

STITCH KEY
☐ Space (sp)
■ Block

Fall Splendor
Doily

DESIGN BY **GEMMA OWEN**

SKILL LEVEL

■■□□

EASY

FINISHED MEASUREMENT

10 inches in diameter

MATERIALS

- Aunt Lydia's Classic Crochet size 10 crochet cotton (350 yds per ball):
  200 yds #431 pumpkin
  100 yds each #341 russet and
  #310 copper mist
  10 yds #423 maize
- Aunt Lydia's Metallic size 10 crochet cotton (100 yds per ball):
  1 ball #1P white/pearl
- Size 7/1.65mm steel crochet hook or size needed to obtain gauge
- Tapestry needle

GAUGE

Flower = 2⅞ inches in diameter; 3 sc = 1 inch;
  4 sc rows = 1 inch

PATTERN NOTES

Weave in loose ends as work progresses.

Join with slip stitch as indicated unless otherwise stated.

SPECIAL STITCHES

Picot: Ch 3, sl st in last st made.

Beginning popcorn (beg pc): Ch 3, 4 dc in same ch-3 sp as beg ch-3, remove lp from hook, insert hook in top of beg ch-3, pick up dropped lp and draw through lp on hook.

Popcorn (pc): 5 dc in ch-3 sp, remove lp from hook, insert hook in first dc of 5-dc group, pick up dropped lp and draw through lp on hook.

Beginning cluster (beg cl): Ch 3, [yo, insert hook in same ch sp, yo, draw through 2 lps on hook] twice, yo, draw through all 3 lps on hook.

Cluster (cl): [Yo, insert hook in ch sp, yo, draw up a lp, yo, draw through 2 lps on hook] 3 times, yo, draw through all 4 lps on hook.

V-stitch (V-st): (Dc, ch 3, dc) in indicated st.

DOILY
CENTER

Rnd 1: With maize, ch 3 *(does not count as first dc)*, 10 dc in 3rd ch from hook, **join** *(see Pattern Notes)* in first dc. *(10 dc)*

Rnd 2: Ch 1, sc in same dc as beg ch-1, ch 1, [sc in next dc, ch 1] around, join in first sc. Fasten off. *(10 sc, 10 ch-1 sps)*

FLOWER

Rnd 3: Join pumpkin in any sc, ch 1, (sc, ch 3, sc) in same sc as beg ch-1, [(sc, ch 3, sc) in next sc] around, join in first sc. *(20 sc, 10 ch-3 sps)*

Rnd 4: Sl st in next ch-3 sp, ch 1, (sc, ch 5, sc) in same ch-3 sp, [(sc, ch 5, sc) in next ch-3 sp] around, do not join.

Rnd 5: [Working behind petals, **bpsc** *(see Stitch Guide)* around each of next 2 sc of rnd 3, ch 4] around, join in first sc.

Rnd 6: Sl st in next ch-4 sp, ch 1, (sc, hdc, 3 dc, hdc, sc) in same ch-4 sp, [(sc, hdc, 3 dc, hdc, sc) in next ch-4 sp] around, do not join.

Rnd 7: Working behind petals, bpsc around sc of rnd 5, ch 5, [bpsc around next sc of rnd 5, ch 5] around, join in first sc.

Rnd 8: Sl st in next ch-5 sp, ch 1, (sc, hdc, 3 dc, hdc, sc) in same ch-5 sp, [(sc, hdc, 3 dc, hdc, sc) in next ch-5 sp] around, do not join.

Rnd 9: Working behind petals, bpsc around each sc of rnd 7, ch 6, [bpsc around next sc of rnd 7, ch 6] around, join in beg sc.

Rnd 10: Sl st in next ch-6 sp, ch 1, (sc, hdc, 3 dc, hdc, sc) in same ch-6 sp, [(sc, hdc, 3 dc, hdc, sc) in next ch-6 sp] around, do not join.

Rnd 11: Working behind petals, bpsc around each sc of rnd 9, ch 7, [bpsc around next sc of rnd 9, ch 7] around, join in first sc.

Rnd 12: Sl st in next ch-7 sp, ch 1, (sc, hdc, 3 dc, hdc, sc) in same ch-7 sp, [(sc, hdc, 3 dc, hdc, sc) in next ch-7 sp] around, do not join.

Rnd 13: Working behind petals, bpsc around next sc of rnd 11, ch 9, [bpsc around next sc of rnd 11, ch 9] around, join in first sc.

Rnd 14: Sl st in next ch-9 sp, ch 1, (sc, hdc, 5 dc, hdc, sc) in same ch-9 sp, [(sc, hdc, 5 dc, hdc, sc) in next ch-9 sp] around, join in first sc. Fasten off.

LEAF
Make 5 each, russet & copper mist.

Rnd 15: Ch 3, 12 dc in 3rd ch from hook, sk beg ch, join in first dc. *(12 dc)*

Rnd 16: Ch 1, (sc, ch 5) in same dc as beg ch-1, sk each of next 2 dc, (sc, ch 5) in next dc, sk each of next 2 dc, sc in next dc, 2 dc in each of next 2 dc, (dc, ch 3, dc) in next dc, 2 dc in each of next 2 dc, join in first sc. *(10 dc, 3 sc, 2 ch-5 sps, 1 ch-3 sp)*

Rnd 17: Ch 1, sc in same sc as beg ch-1, 7 dc in next ch-5 sp, sc in next sc, ch 2, sl st between any 2 sc between petals of rnd 14 of Flower, ch 2, sl st in same sc on leaf, 7 dc in next ch-5 sp, [sc in next dc, ch 2] 4 times, sc in next dc, (2 dc, tr, **picot**—*see Special Stitches*, tr, 2 dc) in next ch-3 sp, [sc in next dc, ch 2] 5 times, sc in next sc, join in first sc. Fasten off.

Continue to rep rnds 15–17, alternating Leaf colors copper and russet, while working Leaves around Flower.

Rnd 18: Join white/pearl in picot at tip of any Leaf, ch 1, (sc, ch 3, sc) in same picot, ch 18, [(sc, ch 3, sc) in picot at tip of next Leaf, ch 18] around, join in first sc. *(10 ch-18 sps, 10 ch-3 sps)*

Rnd 19: Sl st in next ch-3 sp, (sc, ch 3, sc) in next ch-3 sp, ch 7, sk next 5 chs of ch-18, [sc in next ch, ch 7] twice, *(sc, ch 3, sc) in next ch-3 sp, ch 7, [sk next 5 chs of next ch-18, sc in next ch, ch 7] twice, rep from * around, join in first sc. *(30 ch-7 sps, 10 ch-3 sps)*

Rnd 20: Sl st in next ch-3 sp, (**beg pc**—*see Special Stitches*, ch 12, sl st in top of pc) in same ch-3 sp, ch 7, [sc in next ch-7 sp, ch 7] 3 times, *(**pc**—*see Special Stitches*, ch 12, sl st in top of pc) in next ch-3 sp, ch 7, [sc in next ch-7 sp, ch 7] 3 times, rep from * around, join in top of beg pc.

Rnd 21: Sl st in next ch-12 sp, **beg cl** (*see Special Stitches*) in same ch-12 sp, ch 2, (**cl**—*see Special Stitches*, ch 2) 4 times and cl in same ch-12 sp, [sc in next ch-7 sp, ch 7] 3 times, sc in next ch sp, *[(cl, ch 2) 5 times and cl] in next ch-12 sp, [sc in next ch-7 sp, ch 7] 3 times, sc in next ch-7 sp, rep from * around, join in top of beg cl.

Rnd 22: Sl st in next ch-2 sp, (beg cl, ch 2, cl, ch 2) in same ch-2 sp, *cl in next ch-2 sp, (ch 2, cl in next ch-2 sp) twice, ch 2, cl in next ch-2 sp, (ch 2, cl in next ch-2 sp) twice, (sc in next ch-7 sp, ch 7) twice, sc in next ch-7 sp**, (cl in next ch-2 sp, ch 2) twice, rep from * around, ending last rep at **, join in beg cl.

Rnd 23: Sl st in next ch-2 sp, ch 1, sc in same ch-2 sp as beg ch-1, *[ch 5, sc in next ch-2 sp] 6 times, ch 5, sc in next ch-7 sp, ch 2, **V-st** (*see Special Stitches*) in next sc, ch 2, sc in next ch-7 sp, ch 5**, sc in next ch-2 sp, rep from * around, ending last rep at **, join in first sc. Fasten off.

Row 24: Now working in rows, with WS facing, join pumpkin with sc in ch-3 sp of any V-st, ch 12, (sc in same ch-3 sp of V-st, ch 12) twice, sc in same V-st, turn. *(4 sc, 3 ch-12 lps)*

Row 25: With RS facing, sl st in next ch-12 lp, ch 1, (3 sc, 2 hdc, 3 dc, 2 hdc, sc) in same ch-12 lp as beg ch-1, (sc, 2 hdc, 3 dc, 2 hdc, sc) in 2nd ch-12 lp, (sc, 2 hdc, 3 dc, 2 hdc, 3 sc) in 3rd ch-12 lp. Fasten off.

[Rep rows 24 and 25 alternately] 9 times.

FINISHING
Block lightly. ∎

Blue Skies
Doily

DESIGN BY **GEMMA OWEN**

SKILL LEVEL

■■□□
EASY

FINISHED MEASUREMENT
8 inches, unblocked

MATERIALS
- Aunt Lydia's Classic Crochet size 10 crochet cotton (350 yds per ball): 1 ball each #479 bridal blue and #487 dark royal 3 yds #422 golden yellow
- Size 7/1.65mm steel crochet hook or size needed to obtain gauge

 0 LACE

GAUGE
Rnds 1–7 = 3 inches

PATTERN NOTES
Weave in loose ends as work progresses.

Join with slip stitch as indicated unless otherwise stated.

Chain-3 at beginning of round counts as first double crochet unless otherwise stated.

SPECIAL STITCHES
Beginning V-stitch (beg V-st): Ch 6, dc in same sp.

V-stitch (V-st): (Dc, ch 3, dc) in same sp.

Single crochet V-stitch (sc V-st): (Sc, ch 3, sc) in indicated st or sp.

Split double crochet (split dc): [Yo, insert hook in next st or sp, yo and draw through 2 lps on hook] twice, yo and draw through all 3 lps on hook.

Beginning popcorn (beg pc): Ch 3, 3 dc in same sp as beg ch-3, remove lp from hook, insert hook in top of beg ch-3, pick up dropped lp and draw through lp on hook.

Popcorn (pc): 4 dc in indicated st, remove lp from hook, insert hook in first dc of 4-dc group, pick up dropped lp and draw through lp on hook.

DOILY
Rnd 1: With golden yellow ch 2, 8 sc in 2nd ch from hook, **join** (*see Pattern Notes*) in beg sc.

Rnd 2: Ch 1, sc in same st, ch 3, (sc, ch 3) in each rem sc around, join in beg sc. Fasten off. (*8 ch-3 sps*)

Rnd 3: Join dark royal in any ch-3 sp, **ch 3** (*see Pattern Notes*), (2 dc, ch 2) in same sp, (3 dc, ch 2) in each rem ch-3 sp around, join in 3rd ch of beg ch-3.

Rnd 4: Ch 3, dc in same st as beg ch-3, dc in next dc of 3-dc group, 2 dc in last dc of 3-dc group, ch 2, [2 dc in first dc of next 3-dc group, dc in next dc of same 3-dc group, 2 dc in last dc of same 3-dc group, ch 2] around, join in 3rd ch of beg ch-3.

Rnd 5: Ch 3, dc in same st as beg ch-3, dc in each of next 3 dc of next 5-dc group, 2 dc in last dc of 5-dc group, ch 2, [2 dc in first dc of next 5-dc group, dc in each of next 3 dc of same 5-dc group, 2 dc in last dc of same 5-dc group, ch 2] around, join in 3rd ch of beg ch-3.

Rnd 6: Ch 1, sc in same st, sk next 2 dc of next 7-dc group, 9 tr in next dc, sk next 2 dc, sc in last dc of same group, ch 3, [sc in first dc of next group, sk next 2 dc, 9 tr in next dc of same group, sk next 2 dc, sc in last dc of same group, ch 3] around, join in beg sc.

Rnd 7: Ch 1, *sl st in each of next 9 tr, ch 3, rep from * around, join in first sl st. Fasten off.

Rnd 8: Working behind ch-3 sps of rnd 7 and around ch-3 sps of rnd 6 around, join bridal blue in any ch-2 sp of rnd 5, **beg V-st** *(see Special Stitches)* in same ch-2 sp, ch 9, *(**V-st**—*see Special Stitches*, ch 9) in next ch-2 sp of rnd 5, rep from * around, join in 3rd ch of beg ch-6.

Rnd 9: Sl st in ch-3 sp, ch 1, **sc V-st** *(see Special Stitches)* in same sp as beg ch-1, ch 3, [sc V-st in next sp, ch 3] around, join in beg sc. *(16 ch-3 sps, 16 V-sts)*

Rnd 10: Sl st in ch-3 sp, ch 3, (3 dc, ch 2, 4 dc) in same ch-3 sp, (4 dc, ch 2, 4 dc) in ch-3 sp of each rem V-st around, join in 3rd ch of beg ch-3. *(16 points)*

Rnd 11: Sl st in each of next 3 dc and in ch-2 sp, ch 1, sc in same sp, ch 8, [sc in next ch-2 sp, ch 8] around, join in beg sc. *(16 sc, 16 ch-8 sps)*

Rnd 12: Sl st in next ch-8 sp, ch 1, (sc, ch 3) 4 times in same ch-8 sp as beg ch-1, (sc, ch 3) 4 times in each rem ch-8 sp around, join in beg sc. *(64 ch-3 sps)*

Rnd 13: Sl st in each of next 3 chs, next sc and in next ch-3 sp to align the next set of points correctly, ch 3, (3 dc, ch 2, 4 dc) in same sp, ch 3, sc in next ch-3 sp, ch 3, *(4 dc, ch 2, 4 dc) in next ch-3 sp, ch 3, sc in next ch-3 sp, ch 3, rep from * around, join in 3rd ch of beg ch-3. Fasten off. *(16 points)*

Rnd 14: Join dark royal with sc in ch-2 sp of any point, ch 3, sc in same sp as beg ch-3, ch 4, ***split dc** (see Special Stitches)* in next 2 ch-3 sps, ch 4, (sc, ch 3, sc) in ch-2 sp of next point, ch 4, rep from * around, join in beg sc.

Rnd 15: Sl st in next ch-3 sp, ch 6, dc in same sp as beg ch-3, ch 3, *V-st in top of split dc, ch 3, V-st in next ch-3 sp, rep from * around, sk ch-4 sps, join in 3rd ch of beg ch-6. *(32 V-sts, 32 ch-3 sps)*

Rnd 16: Sl st in next ch-3 sp, ch 1, (sc, ch 3, sc) in same sp as beg ch-1, ch 2, sc in next ch-3 sp between V-sts, ch 2, *(sc, ch 3, sc) in next V-st, ch 2, sc in next ch-3 sp between V-sts, ch 2, rep from * around, join in beg sc.

Rnd 17: Sl st in next ch-3 sp, **beg pc** *(see Special Stitches)*, ch 3, sc in next ch-2 sp, ch 2, sc in next ch-2 sp, ch 3, ***pc** (see Special Stitches)* in next ch-3 sp, ch 3, sc in next ch-2 sp, ch 2, sc in next ch-2 sp, ch 3, rep from * around, join in top of beg pc. Fasten off. *(40 pc, 80 ch-2 sps)*

Rnd 18: Join bridal blue with sc in any ch-3 sp before pc, ch 3, sc in next ch-3 sp, ch 3, pc in next ch-2 sp, ch 3, *[sc in next ch-3 sp, ch 3] twice, pc in next ch-2 sp, ch 3, rep from * around, join in beg sc. *(32 pc)*

Rnd 19: Sl st in next ch-3 sp, ch 4 (counts as first tr), 6 tr in same sp, sk next ch-3 sp, sc in top of next pc, sk next ch-3 sp, *7 tr in next ch-3 sp, sk next ch-3 sp, sc in top of next pc, rep from * around, join in beg sc. Fasten off.

FINISHING
Block. ∎

Wood Violet
Doily

DESIGN BY **ELLEN ANDERSON**

SKILL LEVEL

BEGINNER

FINISHED MEASUREMENT
13 inches in diameter

MATERIALS
- Aunt Lydia's Classic Crochet size 10 crochet cotton (350 yds per ball): 250 yds #495 wood violet
- Size 7/1.65mm steel crochet hook or size needed to obtain gauge
- Starch

GAUGE
Rnds 1 and 2 = 1½ inches; 3 shells = 1 inch

Check gauge to save time.

PATTERN NOTES
Weave in loose ends as work progresses.

Join with slip stitch as indicated unless otherwise stated.

SPECIAL STITCHES
Beginning 3-double crochet cluster (beg 3-dc cl):
Ch 2, [yo, insert hook in indicated st, yo, draw up a lp, yo, draw through 2 lps on hook] twice, yo, draw through all 3 lps on hook.

3-double crochet cluster (3-dc cl): [Yo, insert hook in next sp, yo, draw up a lp, yo, draw through 2 lps on hook] three times, yo, draw through all 4 lps on hook.

Shell: [3-dc cl, ch 3, 3-dc cl] in indicated ch sp.

Double shell: [(3-dc cl, ch 3) twice, 3-dc cl] in indicated ch sp.

Note: *When a rnd begs with a shell or double shell, sl st into indicated ch-3 sp, [beg 3-dc cl, ch 3, 3-dc cl] in same sp or [beg 3-dc cl, (ch 3, 3-dc cl) twice] in same sp. Pattern will simply indicate to shell or double shell in indicated ch sp.*

DOILY
Rnd 1 (RS): Ch 8, **join** *(see Pattern Notes)* to form a ring, **ch 3** *(counts as first dc)*, 23 dc in ring, join in 3rd ch of beg ch-3. *(24 dc)*

Rnd 2: **Beg 3-dc cl** *(see Special Stitches)* in first dc, ch 3, sk next dc, [**3-dc cl** *(see Special Stitches)* in next dc, ch 3, sk next dc] rep around, join in top of beg cl. *(12 cls)*

Rnd 3: [**Shell** *(see Special Stitches and Special Stitches Note)* in next ch-3 sp] around, join in top of beg cl. *(12 shells)*

Rnd 4: *Shell in next ch-3 sp, ch 5, [sc, ch 3, sc] in next ch-3 sp, ch 5, rep from * around, join in top of beg cl.

Rnd 5: [Shell in ch-3 sp of next shell, ch 3, sc in next ch-5 sp, ch 5, sc in next ch-5 sp, ch 3] around, join in top of beg cl.

Rnd 6: [Shell in ch-3 sp of next shell, ch 3, 10 dc in next ch-5 sp, ch 3] around, join in top of beg cl. *(6 shells, 6 pineapple bases)*

Rnd 7: *Shell in ch-3 sp of next shell, ch 3, dc in first dc of next 10-dc group, [ch 1, dc in next dc] 9 times, ch 3, rep from * around, join in top of beg cl.

Rnd 8: *Double shell *(see Special Stitches and Special Stitches Note)* in ch-3 sp of next shell, ch 3, sc in next ch-1 sp, [ch 3, sc in next ch-1 sp] 8 times, ch 3, rep from * around, join in top of beg cl.

Rnd 9: *[Shell in ch-3 sp of next shell] twice, ch 3, sk next ch-3 sp, sc in next ch-3 sp, [ch 3, sc in next ch-3 sp] 7 times, ch 3, rep from * around, join in top of beg cl.

Rnd 10: *Shell in ch-3 sp of next shell, ch 5, shell in ch-3 sp of next shell, ch 3, sk next ch-3 sp, sc in next ch-3 sp, [ch 3, sc in next ch-3 sp] 6 times, ch 3, rep from * around, join in top of beg cl.

Rnd 11: *Shell in ch-3 sp of next shell, ch 5, sc in next ch-5 sp, ch 5, shell in ch-3 sp of next shell, ch 3, sk next ch-3 sp, sc in next ch-3 sp, [ch 3, sc in next ch-3 sp] 5 times, ch 3, rep from * around, join in top of beg cl.

Rnd 12: *Shell in ch-3 sp of shell, ch 5, [sc in next ch-5 sp, ch 5] twice, shell in ch-3 sp of next shell, ch 3, sk next ch-3 sp, sc in next ch-3 sp, [ch 3, sc in next ch-3 sp] 4 times, ch 3, rep from * around, join in top of beg cl.

Rnd 13: *Shell in ch-3 sp of shell, ch 5, [sc in next ch-5 sp, ch 5] 3 times, shell in ch-3 sp of next shell, ch 3, sk next ch-3 sp, sc in next ch-3 sp, [ch 3, sc in next ch-3 sp] 3 times, ch 3, rep from * around, join in top of beg cl.

Rnd 14: *Shell in ch-3 sp of next shell, ch 5, [sc in next ch-5 sp, ch 5] 4 times, shell in ch-3 sp of next shell, ch 3, sk next ch-3 sp, sc in next ch-3 sp, [ch 3, sc in next ch-3 sp] twice, ch 3, rep from * around, join in top of beg cl.

Rnd 15: *Shell in ch-3 sp of next shell, ch 5, [sc in next ch-5 sp, ch 5] 5 times, shell in ch-3 sp of next shell, ch 3, sk next ch-3 sp, sc in next ch-3 sp, ch 3, sc in next ch-3 sp, ch 3, rep from * around, join in top of beg cl.

Rnd 16: *Shell in ch-3 sp of next shell, ch 5, [sc in next ch-5 sp, ch 5] 6 times, shell in ch-3 sp of next shell, ch 3, sk next ch-3 sp, sc in next ch-3 sp, ch 3, rep from * around, join in top of beg cl.

Rnd 17: *Shell in ch-3 sp of shell, ch 5, [sc in next ch-5 sp, ch 5] 7 times, shell in ch-3 sp of next shell, rep from * around, join in top of beg cl, turn, sl st into ch-3 sp of last shell, turn.

Rnd 18: Ch 1, draw up a lp in each of next 2 ch-3 sps of shells, yo, draw through all 3 lps on hook *(sc dec made)*, ch 5, [sc in next ch-5 sp, ch 5] 8 times, *draw up a lp in each of next 2 ch-3 sps of shells, yo, draw through all 3 lps on hook *(sc dec made)*, ch 5, [sc in next ch-5 sp, ch 5] 8 times, rep from * around, join in beg sc dec.

Rnd 19: Sl st into center of next ch-5 sp, ch 1, sc in same ch sp as beg ch-1, ch 5, [sc in next ch-5 sp, ch 5] rep around, join in beg sc. *(54 ch-5 sps)*

Rnd 20: Sl st into ch-5 sp, ch 3, 4 dc in same ch-5 sp, [5 dc in next ch-5 sp] rep in each ch-5 sp around, join in 3rd ch of beg ch-3. *(270 dc)*

Rnd 21: Beg 3-dc cl in first st, ch 3, sk next 2 dc, [3-dc cl in next dc, ch 3, sk next 2 dc] rep around, join in top of beg cl. *(90 cls)*

Rnd 22: Sl st into ch-3 sp, beg 3-dc cl, [ch 4, sl st in 3rd ch from hook, ch 1, 3-dc cl] in same ch-3 sp as beg cl, *[3-dc cl, ch 4, sl st in 3rd ch from hook, ch 1, 3-dc cl] in next ch-3 sp, rep from * around, join in top of beg cl. Fasten off.

FINISHING
Starch and press doily. ■

Morning Star
Doily

DESIGN BY **KAREN ROBISON**

SKILL LEVEL

BEGINNER

FINISHED MEASUREMENT

14½ inches in diameter

MATERIALS

- Aunt Lydia's Classic Crochet size 10 crochet cotton (350 yds per ball): 225 yds #428 mint green
- Size 5/1.90mm steel crochet hook or size needed to obtain gauge
- Starch

GAUGE

Rnds 1–6 = 2¾ inches; 4 dc = ½ inches

Check gauge to save time.

PATTERN NOTES

Weave in loose ends as work progresses.

Join rounds with slip stitch unless otherwise stated.

SPECIAL STITCHES

Beginning 2-dc cluster (beg 2-dc cl): Ch 2, dc in next ch-3 sp.

2-double crochet cluster (2-dc cl): [Yo, insert hook in next ch-3 sp, yo, draw up a lp, yo, draw through 2 lps on hook] twice, yo, draw through all 3 lps on hook.

Beginning 3-double crochet cluster (beg 3-dc cl): Ch 2, (yo, insert hook in next dc, yo, draw up a lp through 2 lps on hook) twice, yo, draw through all 3 lps on hook.

Picot: Ch 5, sl st in top of last dc.

3-double crochet cluster (3-dc cl): (Yo, insert hook in next dc, yo, draw through 2 lps on hook) 3 times, yo, draw through all 4 lps on hook.

DOILY

Rnd 1 (RS): Ch 6, **join** (*see Pattern Notes*) to form a ring, ch 10 (*counts as first dc, ch-7 sp*), [dc in ring, ch 7] 5 times, join in 3rd ch of beg ch-10. (*6 dc, 6 ch-7 sps*)

Rnd 2: Ch 1, sc in each dc and each ch around, join in beg sc. (*48 sc*)

Rnd 3: Sl st in next sc, ch 1, [sc in each of next 3 sc, 3 sc in next sc, sc in each of next 3 sc, ch 1, sk next sc] 6 times, join in beg sc. (*54 sc, 6 ch-1 sps*)

Rnd 4: Sl st in next sc, ch 1, [sc in each of next 3 sc, 3 sc in next sc (center sc of 3-sc group), sc in each of next 3 sc, ch 2, sk next 2 sc] 6 times, join in beg sc.

Rnd 5: Sl st in next sc, ch 1, [sc in each of next 3 sc, 3 sc in next sc, sc in each of next 3 sc, ch 2, sk next 2 sc] 6 times, join in beg sc.

Rnd 6: Sl st in next sc, ch 1, [sc in each of next 3 sc, 3 sc in next sc, sc in each of next 3 sc, ch 4, sk next 2 sc] around, join in beg sc.

Rnd 7: Sl st in next sc, ch 1, [sc in each of next 3 sc, 3 sc in next sc, sc in each of next 3 sc, ch 7, sk next 2 sc] 6 times, join in beg sc.

Rnd 8: Sl st in next 2 sc, ch 1, [sc in each of next 2 sc, 3 sc in next sc (center sc of 3-sc group), sc in each of next 2 sc, ch 1, sk next 2 sc, sc in each of next 3 chs, 3 sc in next ch, sc in each of next 3 chs, ch 1, sk next 2 sc] 6 times, join in beg sc.

Rnd 9: Sl st in next sc, ch 1, [sc in next sc, 3 sc in next sc, sc in next sc, ch 2, sk next 3 sc, sc in each of next 3 sc, 3 sc in next sc, sc in each of next 3 sc, ch 2, sk next 3 sc] 6 times, join in beg sc.

Rnd 10: Sl st into center sc of 3-sc group, ch 1, [3 sc in center sc of 3-sc group, ch 3, sk next 3 sc, sc in each of next 3 sc, 3 sc in next sc, sc in each of next 3 sc, ch 3, sk next 3 sc] 6 times, join in beg sc.

Rnd 11: Sl st in next sc, ch 1, sc in center sc of 3-sc group, ch 3, sc in center of next ch-3 sp, ch 3, sk next sc, sc in each of next 3 sc, 3 sc in next sc, sc in each of next 3 sc, ch 3, sc in center of next ch-3 sp, ch 3, [sk next sc, sc in center sc of next 3-sc group, ch 3, sc in center of next ch-3 sp, ch 3, sk next sc, sc in each of next 3 sc, 3 sc in next sc, sc in each of next 3 sc, ch 3, sc in center of next ch-3 sp, ch 3] 5 times, join in beg sc.

Rnd 12: Sl st into center of next ch-3 sp, ch 1, sc in same st as beg ch-1, ch 3, sc in next ch-3 sp, ch 3, sk next sc, sc in each of next 3 sc, 3 sc in next sc, sc in each of next 3 sc, [(ch 3, sc in center of next ch-3 sp) 4 times, ch 3, sk next sc, sc in each of next 3 sc, 3 sc in next sc, sc in each of next 3 sc] 5 times, [ch 3, sc in next ch-3 sp] twice, ch 1, hdc in beg sc to form last ch-3 sp.

Rnd 13: Ch 1, sc in same sp as beg ch-1, [ch 3, sc in next ch-3 sp] twice, ch 3, sk next 2 sc, sc in each of next 2 sc, 3 sc in next sc, sc in each of next 2 sc, [(ch 3, sc in center of next ch-3 sp) 5 times, ch 3, sk next 2 sc, sc in each of next 2 sc, 3 sc in next sc, sc in each of next 2 sc] 5 times, [ch 3, sc in next ch-3 sp] twice, ch 1, hdc in beg sc.

Rnd 14: Ch 1, sc in same sp as beg ch-1, [ch 3, sc in next ch-3 sp] 3 times, ch 3, sk next 2 sc, sc in next sc, 3 sc in next sc, sc in next sc, [(ch 3, sc in center of next ch-3 sp) 6 times, ch 3, sk next 2 sc, sc in next sc, 3 sc in next sc, sc in next sc] 5 times, [ch 3, sc in next ch-3 sp] twice, ch 1, hdc in beg sc.

Rnd 15: Ch 1, sc in same sp as beg ch-1, [ch 3, sc in center of next ch-3 sp] 4 times, ch 3, sk next 2 sc, 3 sc in next sc, [(ch 3, sc in center of next ch-3 sp) 7 times, ch 3, sk next 2 sc, 3 sc in next sc] 5 times, [ch 3, sc in center of next ch-3 sp] twice, ch 1, hdc in beg sc.

Rnd 16: Ch 1, sc in same sp as beg ch-1, [ch 3, sc in center of next ch-3 sp] 5 times, ch 3, sk next sc, sc in next sc, [(ch 3, sc in center of next ch-3 sp) 8 times, ch 3, sk next sc, sc in next sc] 5 times, [ch 3, sc in center of next ch-3 sp] twice, ch 1, hdc in beg sc.

Rnd 17: Ch 1, sc in same sp as beg ch-1, ch 3, [sc in center of next ch-3 sp, ch 3] around, join in beg sc. (*54 ch-3 sps*)

Rnd 18: Ch 1, sc in each sc and each ch around, join in beg sc. (*216 sc*)

Rnd 19: **Ch 6** (*counts as first dc, ch-3 sp*), sk next 3 sc, [dc in next sc, ch 3, sk next 3 sc] around, join in 3rd ch of beg ch-6. (*54 dc, 54 ch-3 sps*)

Rnd 20: Sl st in next ch, **ch 3** (*counts as first dc throughout*), dc in each of next 2 chs, ch 3, sk next dc, [dc in each of next 3 chs, ch 3, sk next dc] around, join in 3rd ch of beg ch-3.

Rnd 21: Sl st into center dc, ch 1, sc in same dc, ch 3, sc in center of next ch-3 sp, [ch 3, sc in center dc of next 3-dc group, ch 3, sc in center of next ch-3 sp] rep around, ending with ch 1, hdc in beg sc.

Rnd 22: Ch 1, sc in same ch sp as beg ch-1, [ch 3, sc in next ch-3 sp] around, ending with ch 1, hdc in beg sc.

Rnd 23: **Beg 2-dc cl** (*see Special Stitches*), ch 5, [**2-dc cl** (*see Special Stitches*), ch 5] around, join in top of beg cl. (*54 cls*)

Rnd 24: Sl st into first ch of ch-5 sp, ch 3, dc in same ch, dc in each of next 3 chs, 2 dc in next ch, ch 6, sk 2-dc cl, sc in next 2-dc cl, ch 6, [sk next ch-5 sp, 2 dc in next ch, dc in each of next 3 chs, 2 dc in next ch, ch 6, sk next 2-dc cl, sc in next 2-dc cl, ch 6] around, join in 3rd ch of beg ch-3. (*18 groups of 7-dc*)

Rnd 25: Ch 3, dc in each of next 6 dc, ch 3, sc in next ch-6 sp, ch 6, sc in next ch-6 sp, ch 3, [dc in each of next 7 dc, ch 3, sc in next ch-6 sp, ch 6, sc in next ch-6 sp, ch 3] around, join in 3rd ch of beg ch-3.

Rnd 26: **Beg 3-dc cl** (*see Special Stitches*), dc in next dc, **picot** (*see Special Stitches*), **3-dc cl** (*see Special Stitches*), ch 9, sc in next ch-6 sp, ch 9, [3-dc cl over next 3 dc, dc in next dc, p, 3-dc cl, ch 9, sc in next ch-6 sp, ch 9] around, join in top of beg cl. Fasten off.

FINISHING
Starch lightly and press. ∎

Autumn Blaze
Table Mat DESIGN BY **SUSAN LOWMAN**

SKILL LEVEL

EASY

FINISHED MEASUREMENT
8¾ inches in diameter

MATERIALS
- Aunt Lydia's Classic Crochet size 10 crochet cotton (350 yds per ball):
    50 yds #196 cardinal
    35 yds #431 pumpkin
    20 yds #421 goldenrod
- Size 7/1.65mm steel crochet hook
- Yarn needle
- ¾-inch bone rings: 49

0
LACE

GAUGE
Gauge is not critical for this project.

PATTERN NOTES
Weave in loose ends as work progresses.

Join with slip stitch as indicated unless otherwise stated.

To join rings together, remove loop from hook, insert hook in indicated stitch and draw dropped loop through stitch.

Rings are crocheted and joined in 7 groups with 7 rings each. Join groups of rings around center group of rings in clockwise direction for right-handed crocheters or in counterclockwise direction for left-handed crocheters.

MAT
CENTER RING
Rnd 1 (RS): Join goldenrod with **sc in ring** *(see illustration)*, 4 sc in ring, ch 1, hdc in ring, ch 1, [5 sc in ring, ch 1, hdc in ring, ch 1] 5 times, **join** *(see Pattern Notes)* in first sc. Fasten off. *(36 sts)*

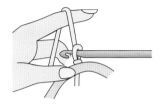
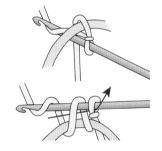

Single Crochet Around Ring

OUTER RING
Rnd 1 (RS): Join pumpkin with sc in new ring, 5 sc in ring, with RS facing, join to center sc of 5-sc between any 2 hdc on Center Ring *(see Pattern Notes)*, 6 sc in same Outer Ring, [6 sc in new ring, join to center sc of 5-sc between next 2 hdc on Center Ring, 6 sc in same Outer Ring] 5 times, join in first sc. Fasten off. *(72 sc)*

FIRST GROUP OF RINGS
Rnd 2 (RS): With RS facing, join cardinal with sc in any Outer Ring, 4 sc in ring, *[ch 1, hdc in ring, ch 1, 5 sc in ring] 3 times**, 5 sc in next Outer Ring, rep from * around, ending last rep at **, join in first sc. Fasten off. *(138 sts)*

2ND GROUP OF RINGS
Rnd 2 (RS): With RS facing, join cardinal with sc in any Outer Ring, 4 sc in ring, *[ch 1, hdc in ring, ch 1, 5 sc in ring] 3 times, 5 sc in next Outer Ring, rep from * 4 times, ch 1, hdc in ring, ch 1, 5 sc in ring, ch 1, join to center hdc on rnd 2 of any ring on Outer Ring on First Group of Rings, hdc in same Outer Ring on current Group of Rings, ch 1, 5 sc in ring,

Continued on page 38

Filet Ruffle
Doily

DESIGN BY **AGNES RUSSELL**

SKILL LEVEL

EASY

FINISHED MEASUREMENTS

Doily center, excluding ruffle, is 10½ inches
in diameter; doily with ruffle is 17 inches
in diameter

MATERIALS

- Aunt Lydia's fine crochet cotton size 20
  (400 yds per ball):
    400 yds #226 natural
- Size 11/1.10mm steel crochet hook or size
  needed to obtain gauge
- Starch

GAUGE

13 sts = 1 inch; 5 rows = 1 inch, before blocking

Check gauge to save time.

PATTERN NOTES

Weave in loose ends as work progresses.

Join rounds with a slip stitch unless
otherwise stated.

SPECIAL STITCHES

Beginning 4-treble crochet cluster (beg 4-tr cl):
Ch 4, [(yo twice, insert hook in next tr, yo,
pull through st, yo, draw through 2 lps on
hook) twice] 3 times, yo, draw through all
lps on hook.

3-picot cluster (3-picot cl): Ch 6, sl st in 6th st
from hook [ch 5, sl st in same st] twice.

Picot (picot): Ch 5, sl st in top of tr.

4-treble crochet cluster (4-tr cl): [Yo twice, insert
hook in next tr, yo, pull through st, (yo, draw
through 2 lps on hook) twice] 4 times, yo, draw
through all lps on hook.

DOILY CENTER

Row 1: Ch 29, dc in 8th ch from hook, [ch 2, sk
next 2 chs, dc in next ch] 7 times, turn. *(8 sps)*

Row 2: Ch 13, dc in 8th ch from hook, ch 2, sk
next 2 chs, dc in next ch, ch 2, dc in next dc (inc
at beg of row), [2 dc in next sp, dc in next dc]
8 times, ch 2, dtr in same st as last dc, [ch 2,
dtr over dtr] twice *(inc at end of row)*, turn.

Row 3: Ch 13, dc in 8th ch from hook, ch 2, sk
next 2 chs, dc in next st, ch 2, dc in next dtr,
[2 dc in next sp, dc in next dtr] twice, 2 dc in
next sp, dc in next dc *(block made)*, [ch 2, sk
next 2 dc, dc in next dc (sp)] 8 times, then work
3 blocks, ch 2, dtr in same st as last dc, [ch 2,
dtr over last dtr made] twice, turn.

Row 4: Ch 11, dc in 8th ch from hook, ch 2, dc in
next dtr, 3 blocks, 14 sps, 3 blocks, inc 2 sps at
end of row, turn.

Follow graph for remainder of rows. To decrease
a space, slip stitch over space or stitches as
indicated by graph. At end of row 48, do not
fasten off.

RUFFLE

Rnd 1: Sc over last dc, [ch 5, sc in next sp]
rep around, ending with ch 1, tr in beg sc to
position hook in center of last ch sp.

Rnd 2: Ch 1, beg in same sp as joining, [4 sc in
next sp, ch 5, {tr, ch 2, 2 tr, ch 2, tr} in next sp,
ch 5] around, *join (see Pattern Notes)* in beg sc.

Rnd 3: Ch 4 *(counts as first tr throughout)*, tr in
each of next 3 sc, * ch 5, tr in next tr, ch 2, 2 tr
in next tr, ch 5 **, tr in each of next 4 sc, rep
from * around, ending last rep at **, join in 4th
ch of beg ch-4.

Continued on page 38

Duck Pond
Doily

DESIGN BY **AGNES RUSSELL**

SKILL LEVEL

■□□□
BEGINNER

FINISHED MEASUREMENTS
11 x 12½ inches

MATERIALS
- Universal Yarn Nazli Gelin Garden size 10 crochet cotton (308 yds per ball):
    1 ball #700-04 deep yellow
- Size 8/1.50mm steel crochet hook or size needed to obtain gauge
- Starch

GAUGE
11 dc = 1 inch; 9 dc rows = 2 inches

PATTERN NOTES
Weave in loose ends as work progresses.

Join with slip stitch as indicated unless otherwise stated.

SPECIAL STITCHES
Block increase (block inc): Ch 5, dc in 4th ch from hook *(beg 3 sk chs count as first dc)*, dc in next ch.

Block: Dc in each of next 3 sts or (2 dc in next ch sp, dc in next st).

Space (sp): (Dc in indicated st, ch 2, sk next 2 sts).

Foundation double crochet block (foundation dc block): Yo, insert hook in top of indicated ch, yo, draw through 1 lp on hook (base st), [yo, draw through 2 lps on hook] twice, *yo, draw up lp in base st, yo draw through 1 lp on hook (base st), [yo, draw through 2 lps on hook] twice, rep from * once.

Block decrease (block dec): Sl st in each of first 3 sts, ch 3, dc in each of next 2 sts.

DOILY
Row 1 (RS): Ch 57, dc in 4th ch from hook, dc in each rem ch across, turn. *(55 dc)*

Row 2 (WS): **Block inc** *(see Special Stitches)*, **block** *(see Special Stitches)*, **sp** *(see Special Stitches)* 16 times, block, dc in top of beg 3 sk chs, **foundation dc block** *(see Special Stitches)*, turn. *(1 block inc, 2 blocks, 16 sps, 1 foundation dc block)*

Rows 3–14: Following chart, work blocks and sps, block inc at beg of each row and foundation dc block at end of each row as indicated, turn at the end of each row.

Rows 15–31: Following chart, work blocks and sps across, turn at end of each row.

Rows 32–44: **Block dec** *(see Special Stitches)*, following chart, work blocks and sps across to last 3 sts, leaving rem sts unworked, turn. Do not fasten off at end of last row.

BORDER
Rnd 1 (RS): Work Border as follows:

A. Ch 5 *(counts as first dc and ch-2)*, sk next 2 dc, sp 17 times, (dc, ch 2, dc) in last dc;

B. working down side of Doily, [(dc, ch 2, dc) in first sl st 1 row below, (dc, ch 2, dc) in 3rd unworked st 1 row below] 6 times, (dc, ch 2, dc) in first sl st 1 row below;

C. [ch 2, dc in top of beg ch-3 1 row below, ch 2, dc in top of last dc 1 row below] 8 times, (ch 2, dc in top of beg ch-3) 1 row below;

D. (ch 2, dc) twice in bottom of beg ch-3 1 row below, [(dc, ch 2, dc) in bottom of last st 1 row

below, (dc, ch 2, dc) in bottom of beg ch-3
1 row below] 6 times, (dc, ch 2, dc) in bottom
of last st 1 row below;

E. working across opposite side of beg ch, [ch 2,
sk 2 chs, dc in next ch] 17 times, (ch 2, dc) twice
in last ch;

F. working up side of Doily, [(dc, ch 2, dc) in
bottom of last st 1 row above, (dc, ch 2, dc) in
bottom of beg ch-3 1 row above] 6 times, (dc,
ch 2, dc) in bottom of last st 1 row above;

G. [ch 2, dc in top of last dc 1 row above, ch 2,
dc in top of beg ch-3 1 row above] 8 times,
(ch 2, dc) in top of last dc 1 row above;

H. (ch 2, dc) twice in top of beg ch-3 1 row above,
[(dc, ch 2, dc) in first sl st 1 row above, (dc,
ch 2, dc) in top of beg ch-3 1 row above] 6 times,
dc in end of last st 1 row above, ch 2, **join** (see
Pattern Notes) in 3rd ch of beg ch-5. (128 ch-2
sps at end of round)

Continued on page 39

Pineapple Fan *Doily*

DESIGN BY **DELLA BIEBER**

SKILL LEVEL

EASY

FINISHED MEASUREMENT
18 inches in diameter

MATERIALS
- Aunt Lydia's Classic Crochet size 10 crochet cotton (400 yds per ball): 260 yds #1 white
- Size 8/1.50mm steel crochet hook or size needed to obtain gauge
- Starch

GAUGE
Rnds 1–4 = 1¾ inches; 4 shell rnds = 1 inch

Take time to check gauge.

PATTERN NOTES
Weave in loose ends as work progresses.

Join with slip stitch as indicated unless otherwise stated.

Chain-3 at beginning of round counts as first double crochet unless otherwise stated.

Work shell in chain-2 space of indicated shell unless otherwise stated.

SPECIAL STITCHES
Beginning shell (beg shell): (Ch 3, dc, ch 2, 2 dc) in indicated st or sp.

Shell: (2 dc, ch 2, 2 dc) in indicated st or sp.

Beginning double shell (beg double shell): (Ch 3, dc, ch 2, shell) in indicated st or sp.

Chain-3 shell (ch-3 shell): (2 dc, ch 3, 2 dc) in indicated st or sp.

Double shell: (Shell, ch 2, 2 dc) in indicated st or sp.

Beginning picot shell (beg picot shell): [Ch 3, dc, (ch 3, sl st in first ch of ch-3), 2 dc in indicated st or sp].

Picot shell: [2 dc, (ch 3, sl st in first ch of ch-3), 2 dc] in indicated st or sp.

DOILY
Rnd 1: Ch 10, **join** *(see Pattern Notes)* in 10th ch from hook to form ring, ch 1, 16 sc in ring, join in beg sc. *(16 sc)*

Rnd 2: Ch 1, sc in same st as beg ch-1, [ch 5, sk next sc, sc in next sc] around, ch 2, dc in beg sc *(counts as last ch-5 sp)*. *(8 sc, 8 ch-5 sps)*

Rnd 3: Ch 1, sc in same ch sp as beg ch-1, ch 5, [sc in next ch-5 sp, ch 5] around, join in beg sc.

Rnd 4: Sl st in next ch sp, **ch 3** *(see Pattern Notes)*, 4 dc in same ch sp as beg ch-3, ch 2, [5 dc in next ch-5 sp, ch 2] around, join in top of beg ch-3. *(40 dc, 8 ch-2 sps)*

Rnd 5: Ch 1, sc in same ch as beg ch-1, ch 7, sk next 3 dc, sc in next dc, [ch 7, sk next ch-2 sp, sc in next dc, ch 7, sk next 3 dc, sc in next dc] around, ch 3, tr in beg sc *(counts as last ch-7 sp)*. *(16 ch-7 sps)*

Rnd 6: Ch 1, sc in same ch sp as beg ch-1, [ch 7, sc in next ch-7 sp] around, ch 3, tr in beg sc *(counts as last ch-7 sp)*.

Rnd 7: Ch 1, sc in same ch sp as beg ch-1, ch 7, [sc in next ch-7 sp, ch 7] around, join in beg sc.

Rnd 8: Sl st in next ch-7 sp, ch 3, 4 dc in same ch sp as beg ch-3, ch 5, sc in next ch sp, ch 5, [5 dc in next ch sp, ch 5, sc in next ch sp, ch 5] around, join in top of beg ch-3. *(40 dc, 8 sc, 16 ch-5 sps)*

Rnd 9: Ch 1, sc in same st as beg ch-1, ch 7, sk next 3 dc, sc in next dc, ch 12, [sc in next dc, ch 7, sk next 3 dc, sc in next dc, ch 12] around, join in beg sc. *(8 ch-7 sps, 7 ch-12 sps, 16 sc)*

Rnd 10: (Sl st, **beg shell** *(see Special Stitches)* in next ch sp, ch 5, [**shell** *(see Special Stitches)* in next ch sp, ch 5] around, join in top of beg ch-3. *(16 shells, 16 ch-5 sps)*

Rnd 11: Beg shell in **next shell** *(see Pattern Notes)*, ch 4, sc in next ch-5 sp, ch 4, [shell in next shell, ch 4, sc in next ch-5 sp, ch 4] around, join in top of beg ch-3. *(16 shells, 32 ch-4 sps, 16 sc)*

Rnd 12: Beg shell in next shell, ch 10, [shell in next shell, ch 10] around, join in top of beg ch-3. *(16 shells, 16 ch-10 sps)*

Rnd 13: Beg double shell *(see Special Stitches)* in next shell, ch 4, sc in next ch-10 sp, ch 4, **ch-3 shell** *(see Special Stitches)* in next shell, ch 4, sc in next ch-10 sp, ch 4, [**double shell** *(see Special Stitches)* in next shell, ch 4, sc in next ch-10 sp, ch 4, ch-3 shell in next shell, ch 4, sc in next ch-10 sp, ch 4] around, join in top of beg ch-3. *(8 double shells, 8 ch-3 shells, 16 sc, 32 ch-4 sps)*

Rnd 14: Beg shell in first ch-2 sp of next double shell, shell in next shell of double shell, ch 6, 6 dc in next ch-3 sp *(pineapple base)*, ch 6, *shell in each of next 2 ch-2 sps of next double shell, ch 6, 6 dc in next ch-3 sp, ch 6, rep from * around, join in top of beg ch-3. (*8 pineapple bases, 16 shells, 16 ch-6 sps*)

Rnd 15: Beg shell in next shell, *ch 2, shell in next shell, ch 4, [2 dc in next dc] 6 times, ch 4**, shell in next shell, rep from * around, ending last rep at **, join in top of beg ch-3. (*96 dc, 16 shells, 16 ch-4 sps, 8 ch-2 sps*)

Rnd 16: Beg shell in next shell, *ch 3, shell in next shell, ch 3, dc in first dc of next 12-dc group, [ch 1, dc in next dc] 11 times, ch 3**, shell in next shell, rep from * around, ending last rep at **, join in top of beg ch-3. (*96 dc, 16 shells, 88 ch-1 sps, 24 ch-3 sps*)

Rnd 17: Beg shell in next shell, ch 3, shell in next shell, ch 3, *sc in next ch-1 sp, [ch 3, sc in next ch-1 sp] 10 times, ch 3**, [shell in next shell, ch 3] twice, rep from * around, ending last rep at **, join in top of beg ch-3. (*88 sc, 16 shells, 104 ch-3 sps*)

Rnd 18: Beg shell in next shell, ch 3, shell in next shell, ch 3, sk next ch-3 sp, sc in next ch-3 sp, [ch 3, sc in next ch-3 sp] 9 times, ch 3**, [shell in next shell, ch 3] twice, rep from * around, ending last rep at **, join in top of beg ch-3. (*80 sc, 16 shells, 96 ch-3 sps*)

Rnd 19: Beg shell in next shell, *shell in next ch-3 sp, shell in next shell, ch 3, sk next ch-3 sp, sc in next ch-3 sp, [ch 3, sc in next ch-3 sp] 8 times, ch 3**, shell in next shell, rep from * around, ending last rep at **, join in top of beg ch-3. (*72 sc, 24 shells, 80 ch-3 sps*)

Rnd 20: Beg shell in next shell, *[ch 2, shell in next shell] twice, ch 3, sk next ch-3 sp, sc in next ch-3 sp, [ch 3, sc in next ch-3 sp] 7 times, ch 3**, shell in next shell, rep from * around, ending last rep at **, join in top of beg ch-3. (*64 sc, 24 shells, 16 ch-2 sps, 72 ch-3 sps*)

Rnd 21: Beg shell in next shell, *[ch 3, shell in next shell] twice, ch 3, sk next ch-3 sp, sc in next ch-3 sp, [ch 3, sc in next ch-3 sp] 6 times, ch 3**, shell in next shell, rep from * around, ending last rep at **, join in top of beg ch-3. (*56 sc, 24 shells, 80 ch-3 sps*)

Rnd 22: Beg shell in next shell, *[shell in next ch-3 sp, shell in next shell] twice, ch 3, sk next ch-3 sp, sc in next ch-3 sp, [ch 3, sc in next ch-3 sp] 5 times, ch 3**, rep from * around, ending last rep at **, join in top of beg ch-3. (*48 sc, 40 shells, 56 ch-3 sps*)

Rnd 23: Beg shell in next shell, *[ch 2, shell in next shell] 4 times, ch 3, sk next ch-3 sp, sc in next ch-3 sp, [ch 3, sc in next ch-3 sp] 4 times, ch 3**, shell in next shell, rep from * around, ending last rep at **, join in top of beg ch-3. (*40 sc, 40 shells, 48 ch-3 sps, 32 ch-2 sps*)

Rnd 24: Beg shell in next shell, *[ch 3, shell in next shell] 4 times, ch 3, sk next ch-3 sp, sc in next ch-3 sp, [ch 3, sc in next ch-3 sp] 3 times, ch 3**, shell in next shell, rep from * around, ending last rep at **, join in top of beg ch-3. (*32 sc, 40 shells, 72 ch-3 sps*)

Rnd 25: Beg shell in next shell, *[shell in next ch-3 sp, shell in next shell] 4 times, ch 3, sk next ch-3 sp, sc in next ch-3 sp, [ch 3, sc in next ch-3 sp] twice, ch 3**, shell in next shell, rep from * around, ending last rep at **, join in top of beg ch-3. (*24 sc, 72 shells, 32 ch-3 sps*)

Rnd 26: Beg shell in next shell, *[ch 1, shell in next shell] 8 times, ch 3, sk next ch-3 sp, sc in next ch-3 sp, ch 3, sc in next ch-3 sp, ch 3**, shell in next shell, rep from * around, ending last rep at **, join in top of beg ch-3. (*16 sc, 72 shells, 24 ch-3 sps, 64 ch-1 sps*)

Rnd 27: Beg shell in next shell, *[ch 3, shell in next shell] 8 times, ch 3, sk next ch-3 sp, sc in next ch-3 sp, ch 3**, shell in next shell, rep from * around, ending last rep at **, join in top of beg ch-3. (*8 sc, 72 shells, 80 ch-3 sps*)

Rnd 28: (Sl st, **beg picot shell**—*see Special Stitches*) in ch-2 sp of next shell, ch 2, sc in next ch-3 sp, ch 2, ***picot shell** (see Special Stitches) in ch-2 sp of next shell, ch 2, sc in next ch-3 sp, ch 2, rep from * around, join in top of beg ch-3. Fasten off. (*72 picot shells, 64 sc, 128 ch-2 sps*)

FINISHING
Starch lightly and press. ∎

Pineapple Pageantry
Centerpiece Doily

DESIGN BY **DELLA BIEBER**

SKILL LEVEL

BEGINNER

FINISHED MEASUREMENT
20 inches in diameter

MATERIALS
- Aunt Lydia's Classic Crochet size 10 crochet cotton (350 yds per ball): 275 yds #422 golden yellow
- Size 7/1.65mm steel crochet hook or size needed to obtain gauge
- Starch

GAUGE
3 shell rnds = 1 inch

Take time to check gauge.

PATTERN NOTES
Weave in loose ends as work progresses.

Join rounds with slip stitch as indicated unless otherwise stated.

SPECIAL STITCHES
Beginning 4-double crochet cluster (beg 4-dc cl): [Ch 3, yo, insert hook in indicated sp, yo, draw up a lp, yo, draw through 2 lps on hook] 3 times, yo, draw through all lps on hook.

4-double crochet cluster (4-dc cl): [Yo, insert hook in indicated sp, yo, draw up a lp, yo, draw through 3 lps on hook] 4 times, yo, draw through all lps on hook.

Shell: (2 dc, ch 1, 2 dc) in indicated sp.

Double Shell: [2 dc, ch 1, 2 dc, ch 1, 2 dc] in indicated space.

Beginning 5-double crochet cluster (beg 5-dc cl): [Ch 3, yo, insert hook in indicated sp, yo, draw up a lp, yo, draw through 2 lps on hook] 4 times, yo, draw through all lps on hook.

5-double crochet cluster (5-dc cl): [Yo, insert hook in indicated sp, yo, draw up a lp, yo, draw through 3 lps on hook] 5 times, yo, draw through all lps on hook.

Picot: Ch 5, sl st in top of dc.

DOILY
Rnd 1: Ch 5, **join** *(see Pattern Notes)* to form a ring, ch 3, dc in ring, ch 1, [2 dc in ring, ch 1] 7 times, join in 3rd ch of beg ch-3. *(16 dc)*

Rnd 2: Ch 3, dc in next dc, ch 3, [dc in each of next 2 dc, ch 3] around, join in 3rd ch of beg ch-3.

Rnd 3: Ch 3, dc in next dc, ch 2, 2 dc in next ch sp, ch 2, [dc in each of next 2 dc, ch 2, 2 dc in next ch sp, ch 2] around, join in 3rd ch of beg ch-3.

Rnd 4: Sl st to center of ch sp, **beg 4-dc cl** *(see Special Stitches)* over same ch sp, ch 5, [**4-dc cl** *(see Special Stitches)* in next ch sp, ch 5] around, join in top of beg cl.

Rnd 5: Rep rnd 4, working ch 8 between each cl instead of ch 5.

Rnd 6: Rep rnd 4, working ch 10 between each cl instead of ch 5.

Rnd 7: Rep rnd 4, working ch 12 between each cl instead of ch 5.

Rnd 8: Ch 1, *[7 sc, ch 4, 7 sc] in next ch sp, rep from * around. Fasten off.

Rnd 9: Join thread in any ch-4 sp, ch 1, sc in same ch sp, ch 15, [sc in next ch-4 sp, ch 15] around, join in beg sc.

Rnd 10: Sl st in ch sp, ch 3, 2 dc, (ch 1, 3 dc) 4 times in same ch sp, *[3 dc, (ch 1, 3 dc) 4 times] in next ch sp, rep from * around, join in 3rd ch of beg ch-3.

Rnd 11: Sl st to next ch-1 sp, ch 1, sc in same ch sp, [ch 5, sc in next ch-1 sp] around, ending with ch 2, dc in beg sc. *(64 ch sps)*

Rnds 12 & 13: Ch 1, sc in same ch sp, [ch 5, sc in next ch sp] around, ending with ch 2, dc in beg sc.

Rnd 14: Ch 1, sc in same ch sp, [ch 5, sc in next ch sp] twice, *ch 2, **shell** *(see Special Stitches)* in next ch sp, ch 2, sc in next ch sp, [ch 5, sc in next ch sp] 6 times, rep from * around, ending with ch 2, dc in beg sc.

Rnd 15: Ch 1, sc in ch sp, [ch 5, sc in next ch sp] twice, *ch 5, [2 dc, ch 4, 2 dc] in next shell, [ch 5, sc in next ch-5 sp] 6 times, rep from * around, ending with [ch 5, sc in next ch-5 sp] 3 times, ch 2, dc in beg sc.

Rnd 16: Ch 1, sc in ch sp, ch 5, *sc in next ch-5 sp, ch 3, shell in next ch-5 sp, ch 5, 9 dc in next ch-4 sp, ch 5, sk next ch-5 sp, shell in next ch-5 sp, ch 3, [sc in next ch-5 sp, ch 5] twice, rep from * around, ending with ch 2, dc in beg sc.

Rnd 17: Ch 1, sc in ch sp, ch 5, sc in next ch sp, *ch 5, shell in ch-1 sp of next shell, ch 5, [dc in next dc, ch 1] 8 times, dc in next dc, ch 5, shell in ch-1 sp of next shell, sk next ch-3 sp, [ch 5, sc in next ch sp] twice, rep from * around, ending with ch 5, join in beg sc.

Rnd 18: Sl st in each of next 2 chs, ch 1, sc in same sp, *ch 7, shell in shell, ch 5, [sc in next ch-1 sp, ch 3] 7 times, sc in next ch-1 sp, ch 5, shell in shell, ch 7, sk next sp, sc in next ch sp, rep from * around, ending with ch 7, join in beg sc.

Rnd 19: **Ch 10** *(counts as first dc, ch-7 sp)*, *shell in shell, ch 5, [sc in next ch-3 sp, ch 3] 6 times, sc in next ch-3 sp, ch 5, shell in shell, ch 7, dc in next sc, ch 7, rep from * around, ending with ch 7, join in 3rd ch of beg ch-10.

Rnd 20: **Ch 6** *(counts as first dc, ch 3)*, dc in same st, *ch 7, shell in shell, ch 5, [sc in next ch-3 sp, ch 3] 5 times, sc in next ch-3 sp, ch 5, shell in shell, ch 7, [dc, ch 3, dc] in next dc, rep from * around, ending with ch 7, join in 3rd ch of beg ch-6.

Rnd 21: Sl st in ch-3 sp, ch 3, 4 dc in same sp, *ch 7, shell in shell, ch 5, [sc in next ch-3 sp, ch 3] 4 times, sc in next ch-3 sp, ch 5, shell in shell, ch 7, 5 dc in next ch-3 sp, rep from * around, ending with ch 7, join in 3rd ch of beg ch-3.

Rnd 22: Ch 3, dc in next dc, 2 dc in next dc, dc in each of next 2 dc, ch 7, **double shell** *(see Special Stitches)* in next shell, ch 5, [sc in next ch-3 sp, ch 3] 3 times, sc in next ch-3 sp, ch 5, double shell in shell, ch 7, *dc in each of next 2 dc, 2 dc in next dc, dc in each of next 2 dc, ch 7, double shell in shell, ch 5, [sc in next ch-3 sp, ch 3] 3 times, sc in next ch-3 sp, ch 5, double shell in shell, ch 7, rep from * around, join in 3rd ch of beg ch-3.

Rnd 23: Ch 3, dc in each of next 5 dc, *ch 7, [shell in shell] twice, ch 5, [sc in next ch-3 sp, ch 3] twice, sc in next ch-3 sp, ch 5, [shell in shell] twice, ch 7, dc in each of next 6 dc, rep from * around, ending with ch 7, join in 3rd ch of beg ch-3.

Rnd 24: Ch 3, dc in each of next 5 dc, *ch 7, shell in shell, ch 3, shell in shell, ch 5, sc in next ch-3 sp, ch 3, sc in next ch-3 sp, ch 5, shell in shell, ch 3, shell in shell, ch 7, dc in each of next 6 dc, rep from * around, ending with ch 7, join in 3rd ch of beg ch-3.

Rnd 25: Ch 3, dc in next dc, **dc dec** *(see Stitch Guide)* in next 2 dc, dc in each of next 2 dc, *ch 7, shell in shell, ch 4, sc in next ch-3 sp, ch 4, shell in shell, ch 5, sc in next ch-3 sp, ch 5, shell in shell, ch 4, sc in next ch-3 sp, ch 4, shell in

Continued on page 39

Sweet Little Whirls
Doily

DESIGN BY **HAZEL HENRY**

SKILL LEVEL

◼☐☐☐
BEGINNER

FINISHED MEASUREMENT

10½ inches in diameter

MATERIALS

- Aunt Lydia's Classic Crochet size 10 crochet cotton (350 yds per ball): 100 yds #226 natural
- Size 7/1.65mm steel crochet hook or size needed to obtain gauge
- Starch

GAUGE

4 dc rnds = 1 inch; ({dc, ch 1} 6 times, dc) = 1 inch

Check gauge to save time.

PATTERN NOTES

Weave in loose ends as work progresses.

Join rounds with a slip stitch as indicated unless otherwise indicated.

SPECIAL STITCH

Picot: Ch 6, sl st in 5th ch from hook.

DOILY

Rnd 1 (RS): Ch 9, **join** (see Pattern Notes) to form a ring, ch 3 (*counts as first dc throughout*), 27 dc in ring, join in 3rd ch of beg ch-3. (*28 dc*)

Rnd 2: Ch 1, sc in same st as beg ch-1, [ch 7, sk 3 dc, sc in next dc] 6 times, ch 7, join in beg sc. (*7 ch lps*)

Rnd 3: Sl st into ch lp, ch 3, [2 dc, ch 3, 3 dc] in same ch lp as beg ch-3, *[3 dc, ch 3, 3 dc] in next ch lp, rep from * around, join in 3rd ch of beg ch-3. (*42 dc, 7 ch-3 sps*)

Rnd 4: Sl st into ch-3 sp, ch 6 (*counts as first dc, ch-3*), 3 dc in same ch lp, ch 7, *[dc, ch 3, 3 dc] in next ch-3 sp, ch 7, rep from * around, join in 3rd ch of beg ch-6.

Rnd 5: Sl st into ch-3 sp, ch 4 (*counts as first dc, ch-1 sp throughout*), [dc, ch 1, dc] in same ch-3 sp, ch 1, sk 1 dc, dc in next dc, ch 1, sk 1 dc, dc in first ch of ch-7 lp, ch 7, *[dc, ch 1, dc, ch 1, dc] in next ch-3 sp, ch 1, sk next dc, dc in next dc, ch 1, sk next dc, dc in first ch of ch-7 lp, ch 7, rep from * around, join in 3rd ch of beg ch-4.

Rnd 6: Sl st into ch-1 sp, ch 4, dc in next ch-1 sp, [ch 1, dc in next ch-1 sp] twice, ch 7, sk first 4 chs of ch-7 lp, dc in next ch, [ch 1, dc in next ch] twice, *[ch 1, sk next dc, dc in ch-1 sp] 4 times, ch 7, sk first 4 chs of ch-7 lp, dc in next ch, [ch 1, dc in next ch] twice, rep from * around, ending with ch 1, join in 3rd ch of beg ch-4.

Rnd 7: Sl st into ch-1 sp, ch 4, dc in next ch-1 sp, ch 1, dc in next ch-1 sp, *ch 7, sk first 4 chs of ch-7 lp, dc in next ch, [ch 1, dc in next ch] twice**, [ch 1, sk next dc, dc in next ch-1 sp] 6 times, rep from * around, ending last rep at **, [ch 1, sk next dc, dc in next ch-1 sp] 3 times, ch 1, join in 3rd ch of beg ch-4.

Rnd 8: Sl st into ch-1 sp, ch 4, dc in next ch-1sp, *ch 7, sk first 4 chs of ch-7 lp, dc in next ch, [ch 1, dc in next ch] twice**, [ch 1, sk next dc, dc in next ch-1 sp] 8 times, rep from * around, ending last rep at **, [ch 1, sk next dc, dc in next ch-1 sp] 6 times, ch 1, join in 3rd ch of beg ch-4.

Rnd 9: Sl st into ch-1 sp, ch 10 (counts as first dc, ch-7 sp), *sk first 4 chs of next ch-7 lp, dc in next ch, [ch 1, dc in next ch] twice**, [ch 1, sk next dc, dc in next ch-1 sp] 10 times, ch 7, rep from * around, ending last rep at **, [ch 1, sk next dc, dc in next ch-1 sp] 9 times, ch 1, join in 3rd ch of beg ch-10.

Rnd 10: Sl st in each of next 2 chs, ch 3, 2 dc in same ch lp as beg ch-3, *ch 5, dc in next ch-1 sp, [ch 1, dc in next ch-1 sp] 10 times, ch 5, sk next ch-1 sp**, 3 dc in next ch-7 lp, rep from * around, ending last rep at **, join in 3rd ch of beg ch-3.

Rnd 11: Ch 3, dc in same st as beg ch-3, *ch 3, sk next dc, 2 dc in next dc, ch 5, sk ch-5 lp, dc in next ch-1 sp, [ch 1, dc in next ch-1 sp] 8 times, ch 5, sk ch-5 lp**, 2 dc in next dc, rep from * around, ending last rep at **, join in 3rd ch of beg ch-3.

Rnd 12: Ch 3, *2 dc in next dc, ch 5, sk ch-3 sp, 2 dc in next dc, dc in next dc, ch 5, sk ch-5 lp, dc in next ch-1 sp, [ch 1, dc in next ch-1 sp] 6 times, ch 5, sk next ch-5 lp**, dc in next dc, rep from * around, ending last rep at **, join in 3rd ch of beg ch-3.

Rnd 13: Ch 3, *dc in each of next 2 dc, ch 3, [3 dc, ch 3, 3 dc] in ch-5 lp, ch 3, dc in each of next 3 dc, ch 5, sk ch-5 lp, dc in next ch-1 sp, [ch 1, dc in next ch-1 sp] 4 times, ch 5, sk ch-5 lp**, dc in next dc, rep from * around, ending last rep at **, join in 3rd ch of beg ch-3.

Rnd 14: Ch 3, dc in each of next 2 dc, *ch 5, sk ch-3 lp and next 3 dc, [3 dc, ch 3, 3 dc] in next ch-3 lp, ch 5, sk 3 dc and next ch-3 lp, dc in each of next 3 dc, ch 6, dc in next ch-1 sp, [ch 1, dc in next ch-1 sp] twice, ch 6, sk next ch-5 lp**, dc in each of next 3 dc, rep from * around, ending last rep at **, join in 3rd ch of beg ch-3.

Rnd 15: Ch 3, dc in same st as beg ch-3, *ch 3, sk next dc, 2 dc in next dc, ch 3, sk ch-5 lp, 2 dc in next dc, ch 3, sk next dc, 2 dc in next dc, ch 3, sk ch-3 lp, 2 dc in next dc, ch 3, sk next dc, 2 dc in next dc, ch 3, sk next dc, 2 dc in next dc, ch 3, sk next dc, 2 dc in next dc, ch 6, sk ch-6 lp, dc in next ch-1 sp, ch 6, sk next ch-6 lp**, 2 dc in next dc, rep from * around, ending last rep at **, join in 3rd ch of beg ch-3.

Rnd 16: Sl st into ch-3 lp, ch 3, [dc, ch 3, 2 dc] in same ch lp as beg ch-3, *ch 5, sk next ch-3 lp, [(2 dc, ch 3, 2 dc) in next ch-3 lp] 3 times, ch 5, sk next ch-3 lp, [2 dc, ch 3, 2 dc] in next ch-3 lp, ch 3, sk ch-6 lp, [2 dc, ch 3, 2 dc] in next dc, ch 3, sk next ch-6 lp**, [2 dc, ch 3, 2 dc] in next ch-3 lp, rep from * around, ending last rep at **, join in 3rd ch of beg ch-3.

Rnd 17: Sl st into ch-3 lp, ch 3, [dc, ch 3, 2 dc] in same ch-3 lp as beg ch-3, *ch 6, sk next ch-5 lp, [2 dc, ch 3, 2 dc] in next ch-3 lp, [(2 dc, ch 3) twice, 2 dc] in next ch-3 lp, [2 dc, ch 3, 2 dc] in next ch-3 lp, ch 6, sk next ch-5 lp, [2 dc, ch 3, 2 dc] in next ch-3 lp, sk next ch-3 lp, [(2 dc, ch 3) twice, 2 dc] in next ch-3 lp, sk next ch-3 lp**, [2 dc, ch 3, 2 dc] in next ch-3 lp, rep from * around, ending last rep at **, join in 3rd ch of beg ch-3.

Rnd 18: Sl st into center ch of ch-3 lp, ch 1, sc in same ch lp as beg ch-1, *ch 7, sc in next ch-6 lp, ch 5, [2 dc, ch 3, 2 dc] in next ch-3 lp, ch 5, tr in next ch-3 lp, **picot** (*see Special Stitch*), ch 1, tr in next ch-3 lp, ch 5, [2 dc, ch 3, 2 dc] in next ch-3 lp, ch 5, sc in next ch-6 lp, ch 7, sc in next ch-3 lp, ch 7, tr in next ch-3 lp, picot, ch 1, tr in next ch-3 lp, ch 7**, sc in next ch-3 lp, rep from * around, ending last rep at **, join in beg sc. Fasten off.

FINISHING

Starch and press doily. ∎

Hearts Aplenty
Table Runner

DESIGN BY
JOYCE GEISLER

SKILL LEVEL

BEGINNER

FINISHED MEASUREMENTS
13 inches wide x 33½ inches long

MATERIALS
- Aunt Lydia's Classic Crochet size 10 crochet cotton (350 yds per ball):
  3 balls #401 orchid pink
- Size 7/1.65mm steel crochet hook or size needed to obtain gauge
- Tapestry needle
- Heavy spray starch

GAUGE
4 sps = 1 inch; 4 rows = 1 inch

PATTERN NOTES
Weave in loose ends as work progresses.

Chain-5 at beginning of row counts as first double crochet and chain 2 unless otherwise stated.

Join with slip stitch as indicated unless otherwise stated.

Chain-3 at beginning of round counts as first double crochet unless otherwise stated.

SPECIAL STITCHES
Block: Dc in each of next 2 sts, dc in next dc.

Space (sp): Ch 2, sk next 2 sts, dc in next dc.

Picot: Ch 3, sl st in first ch of ch-3.

RUNNER
Row 1 (RS): Ch 146, dc in 8th ch from hook (*7 sk chs count as first dc, ch 2, sk 2 chs*), [ch 2, sk next 2 chs, dc in next ch] across, turn. (*47 sps*)

Row 2: **Ch 5** (*see Pattern Notes*), sk next 2 sts, dc in next dc, [**block** (*see Special Stitches*), **sp** (*see Special Stitches*)] 22 times, block, ch 2, sk next 2 chs, dc in next ch of beg sk chs. (*23 blocks, 24 sps*)

Row 3: Ch 5, sk next 2 sts, dc in next dc, [sp, block] 22 times, sp, ch 3, dc in 3rd ch of beg ch-5, turn. (*22 blocks, 25 sps*)

Rows 4–23: Following chart, ch 5, work blocks and sps across each row, turn.

STITCH KEY
☒ Block
☐ Space (sp)

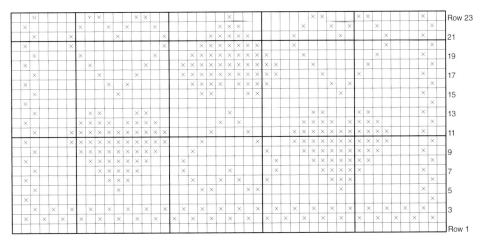

Hearts-a-Plenty Table Runner
Chart

Rows 24–143: [Rep rows 4–23 consecutively] 6 times.

Rows 144–153: Rep rows 4–13.

Row 154: Rep row 4.

Row 155: Rep row 3.

Row 156: Rep row 2.

Row 157: Ch 5, dc in next dc, [sp] 45 times, ch 2, sk 2 chs, dc in next ch of beg ch-5. Fasten off. *(47 sps)*

BORDER
Rnd 1 (RS): **Join** *(see Pattern Notes)* in any corner sp, **ch 3** *(see Pattern Notes)*, 2 dc in same sp, ***picot** *(see Special Stitches)*, sk next sp, [3 dc in next sp, picot, sk next sp] across to next corner, (3 dc, picot, 3 dc) in corner sp, rep from * around, ending with (3 dc, picot) in same corner as beg ch 3, join in beg ch-3. Fasten off.

FINISHING
Starch and block to measurements. ■

PEACOCK DOILY
Continued from page 5

Row 19: Ch 3, [**dc dec** *(see Stitch Guide)* in next 2 sts] twice, dc in next dc. Fasten off. *(4 dc)*

HEAD CREST
Row 1: Thread 5 blue beads on white, and using size 10 hook, join in center st at top of head, ch 1, sc in same st, [ch 5, push up a bead, ch 1 over bead, ch 5, sc in same st on head] 5 times. Fasten off.

FINISHING
For eye, thread embroidery needle with doubled strand of white cotton and make an 18-wrap bullion stitch near center of head about ¼ inch down from the top. Tack center of st down so it curves to the right. Sew 3mm black bead to inside curve of bullion stitch for eye.

For beak, sew tubular black beads to left side of head for beak, leaving a little space between them so beak is pointed.

Sew Body to Tail using sewing needle and thread. Steam-press Peacock. ■

BIRDS OF A FEATHER DOILY
Continued from page 6

RUNNER
Row 1 (RS): Ch 169, dc in 4th ch from hook *(3 sk chs count as first dc)*, dc in each of next 2 chs, [**sp** *(see Special Stitches)*, **block** *(see Special Stitches)*] 27 times, turn. *(28 blocks, 27 sps)*

Row 2: **Beg block inc** *(see Special Stitches)*, sp, [block, sp] across, ending with **end block inc** *(see Special Stitches)*, turn. *(29 blocks, 28 sps)*

Rows 3–29: Following chart, work blocks and sps as indicated. At the end of last rep, fasten off.

FINISHING
Block Runner to finished measurements. ■

AUTUMN BLAZE TABLE MAT
Continued from page 21

ch 1, hdc in ring, ch 1, 5 sc in ring, join in first sc. Fasten off. *(138 sts)*

3RD–6TH GROUP OF RINGS

Rnd 2 (RS): With RS facing, join cardinal with sc in any Outer Ring, 4 sc in ring, *[ch 1, hdc in ring, ch 1, 5 sc in ring] 3 times, 5 sc in next Outer Ring, rep from * 3 times, ch 1, hdc in ring, ch 1, 5 sc in ring, ch 1, join to center hdc of first Outer Ring worked on rnd 2 of Outer Rings on last Group of Rings made, hdc in same Outer Ring on current Group of Rings, ch 1, 5 sc in ring, ch 1, hdc in ring, ch 1, 5 sc in ring, 5 sc in next Outer Ring, ch 1, hdc in ring, ch 1, 5 sc in ring, ch 1, join to center hdc of next ring on rnd 2 of Outer Rings on First Group of Rings, hdc in same outer ring on current Group of Rings, ch 1, 5 sc in ring, ch 1, hdc in ring, ch 1, 5 sc in ring, join to first sc. Fasten off. *(138 sts)*

7TH GROUP OF RINGS

Rnd 2 (RS): With RS facing, join cardinal with sc in any Outer Ring, 4 sc in ring, *[ch 1, hdc in ring, ch 1, 5 sc in ring] 3 times, 5 sc in next Outer Ring, rep from * twice, ch 1, hdc in ring, ch 1, 5 sc in ring, ch 1, join to center hdc of first Outer Ring worked on rnd 2 of Outer Rings on last Group of Rings made, hdc in same Outer Ring on current Group of Rings, ch 1, 5 sc in ring, ch 1, hdc in ring, ch 1, 5 sc in ring, 5 sc in next Outer Ring, ch 1, hdc in ring, ch 1, 5 sc in ring, ch 1, join to center hdc of next ring on rnd 2 of Outer Rings on First Group of Rings, hdc in same Outer Ring on current Group of Rings, ch 1, 5 sc in ring, ch 1, hdc in ring, ch 1, 5 sc in ring, 5 sc in next Outer Ring, ch 1, hdc in ring, ch 1, 5 sc in ring, ch 1, join to center hdc of 5th Outer Ring worked on rnd 2 of Outer Rings on 2nd Group of Rings, hdc in same Outer Ring on current Group of Rings, ch 1, 5 sc in ring, ch 1, hdc in ring, ch 1, 5 sc in ring, join to first sc. Fasten off. *(138 sts)*

FINISHING

Block to measurement. ■

FILET RUFFLE DOILY
Continued from page 22

Rnds 4–8: Ch 4, tr in each of next 3 tr, [ch 9, tr in next tr, ch 2, tr in each of next 4 tr, ch 2, tr in next tr, ch 9 *, tr in each of next 4 tr] around, ending last rep at *, join in 4th ch of beg ch-4.

Rnd 9: Beg 4-tr cl *(see Special Stitches)*, **3-picot cl** *(see Special Stitches)*, ch 9, tr in next tr, **picot** *(see Special Stitches)*, ch 3,* [4-tr cl *(see Special Stitches)*, 3-picot cl, ch 3, tr in next tr, picot, ch 9, *4-tr cl, 3-picot cl, ch 9, tr in next tr, picot, ch 3, rep from * around, join in 4th ch of beg ch-4. Fasten off.

FINISHING

Starch doily, allow to dry completely and press ruffle. ■

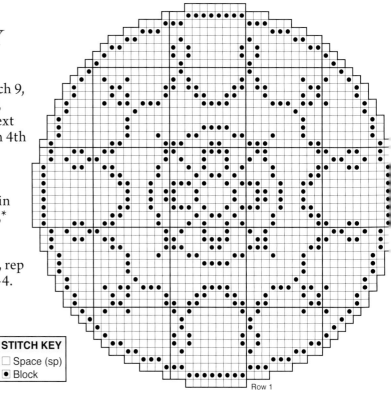

Row 1

Filet Ruffle Doily
Doily Center

DUCK POND DOILY

Continued from page 25

Rnd 2: Sl st in next ch-2 sp, ch 1, sc in same ch-2 sp, 5 dc in next ch-2 sp, [sc in next ch-2 sp, 5 dc in next ch-2 sp] around, join in beg sc. (*64 groups of 5 dc*)

Rnd 3: *Ch 4, [sl st, ch 3, sl st] in 3rd dc of next 5-dc group, ch 4, sl st in next sc, rep from * around. Fasten off.

FINISHING
Starch and block to measurements. ■

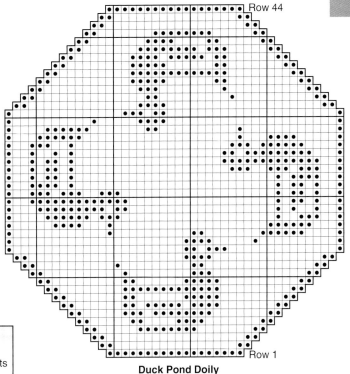

Duck Pond Doily
Duck Pond Chart

STITCH KEY	
●■●□	Dc in each of next 7 sts, ch 2, sk 2 sts, dc in next st
●■●□	Dc in each of next 4 sts, ch 2, sk 2 sts, dc in each of next 4 sts
□□□	Dc in next st, [ch 2, sk 2 sts, dc in next st] 3 times

PINEAPPLE PAGEANTRY CENTERPIECE DOILY

Continued from page 31

shell, ch 7, dc in each of next 2 dc, dc dec in next 2 dc, dc in each of next 2 dc, rep from * around, ending with ch 7, join in 3rd ch of beg ch-3.

Rnd 26: **Beg 5-dc cl** (*see Special Stitches*) over next 5 dc, *ch 10, shell in shell, [ch 4, sc in next ch sp] twice, ch 4, shell in shell, ch 3, shell in shell, [ch 4, sc in next ch sp] twice, ch 4, shell in shell, ch 10, **5-dc cl** (*see Special Stitches*) over next 5 dc, rep from * around, ending with ch 10, join in top of beg cl.

Rnd 27: Ch 13, *shell in shell, ch 5, sk next ch-4 sp, shell in next ch sp, ch 5, [shell in shell] twice, ch 5, sk next ch-4 sp, shell in next sp, ch 5, shell in shell, ch 10, dc in top of next cl,

ch 10, rep from * around, ending with ch 10, join in 3rd ch of beg ch-13.

Rnd 28: Ch 3, dc in same st, **picot** (*see Special Stitches*), 2 dc in same ch sp, *ch 5, sc in next ch sp, ch 5, [2 dc, picot, 2 dc] in next shell, **ch 3, sc in next ch sp, ch 3, [2 dc, picot, 2 dc] in next shell**, rep from ** to ** once, [2 dc, ch-5 picot, 2 dc] in next shell, rep from ** to ** twice, ch 5, sc in next ch sp, ch 5, [2 dc, ch-5 ,picot, 2 dc] in top of next dc, rep from * around, ending with ch 5, join in 3rd ch of beg ch-3. Fasten off.

FINISHING
Starch and block to measurement. ■

Annie's® *A Baker's Dozen Easy Crochet Doilies* is published by Annie's, 306 East Parr Road, Berne, IN 46711. Printed in USA. Copyright © 2014 Annie's. All rights reserved. This publication may not be reproduced in part or in whole without written permission from the publisher.

RETAIL STORES: If you would like to carry this pattern book or any other Annie's publication, visit AnniesWSL.com.

Every effort has been made to ensure that the instructions in this pattern book are complete and accurate. We cannot, however, take responsibility for human error, typographical mistakes or variations in individual work. Please visit AnniesCustomerCare.com to check for pattern updates.

ISBN: 978-1-59635-996-3
3 4 5 6 7 8 9

STITCH GUIDE

FOR MORE COMPLETE INFORMATION,
VISIT **ANNIESCATALOG.COM/STITCHGUIDE**

STITCH ABBREVIATIONS

beg	begin/begins/beginning
bpdc	back post double crochet
bpsc	back post single crochet
bptr	back post treble crochet
CC	contrasting color
ch(s)	chain(s)
ch-	refers to chain or space previously made (i.e., ch-1 space)
ch sp(s)	chain space(s)
cl(s)	cluster(s)
cm	centimeter(s)
dc	double crochet (singular/plural)
dc dec	double crochet 2 or more stitches together, as indicated
dec	decrease/decreases/decreasing
dtr	double treble crochet
ext	extended
fpdc	front post double crochet
fpsc	front post single crochet
fptr	front post treble crochet
g	gram(s)
hdc	half double crochet
hdc dec	half double crochet 2 or more stitches together, as indicated
inc	increase/increases/increasing
lp(s)	loop(s)
MC	main color
mm	millimeter(s)
oz	ounce(s)
pc	popcorn(s)
rem	remain/remains/remaining
rep(s)	repeat(s)
rnd(s)	round(s)
RS	right side
sc	single crochet (singular/plural)
sc dec	single crochet 2 or more stitches together, as indicated
sk	skip/skipped/skipping
sl st(s)	slip stitch(es)
sp(s)	space(s)/spaced
st(s)	stitch(es)
tog	together
tr	treble crochet
trtr	triple treble crochet
WS	wrong side
yd(s)	yard(s)
yo	yarn over

YARN CONVERSION

OUNCES TO GRAMS		GRAMS TO OUNCES	
1	28.4	25	⅞
2	56.7	40	1⅔
3	85.0	50	1¾
4	113.4	100	3½

UNITED STATES		UNITED KINGDOM
sl st (slip stitch)	=	sc (single crochet)
sc (single crochet)	=	dc (double crochet)
hdc (half double crochet)	=	htr (half treble crochet)
dc (double crochet)	=	tr (treble crochet)
tr (treble crochet)	=	dtr (double treble crochet)
dtr (double treble crochet)	=	ttr (triple treble crochet)
skip	=	miss

Single crochet decrease (sc dec): (Insert hook, yo, draw lp through) in each of the sts indicated, yo, draw through all lps on hook.

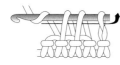

Example of 2-sc dec

Half double crochet decrease (hdc dec): (Yo, insert hook, yo, draw lp through) in each of the sts indicated, yo, draw through all lps on hook.

Example of 2-hdc dec

Reverse single crochet (reverse sc): Ch 1, sk first st, working from left to right, insert hook in next st from front to back, draw up lp on hook, yo and draw through both lps on hook.

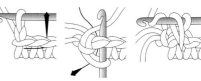

Chain (ch): Yo, pull through lp on hook.

Single crochet (sc): Insert hook in st, yo, pull through st, yo, pull through both lps on hook.

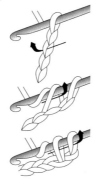

Double crochet (dc): Yo, insert hook in st, yo, pull through st, [yo, pull through 2 lps] twice.

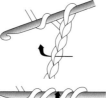

Double crochet decrease (dc dec): (Yo, insert hook, yo, draw lp through, yo, draw through 2 lps on hook) in each of the sts indicated, yo, draw through all lps on hook.

Example of 2-dc dec

Front loop (front lp) Back loop (back lp)

Front Loop   Back Loop

Front post stitch (fp): Back post stitch (bp): When working post st, insert hook from right to left around post of st on previous row.

Back   Front

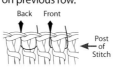

Post of Stitch

Half double crochet (hdc): Yo, insert hook in st, yo, pull through st, yo, pull through all 3 lps on hook.

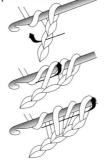

Double treble crochet (dtr): Yo 3 times, insert hook in st, yo, pull through st, [yo, pull through 2 lps] 4 times.

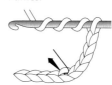

Treble crochet decrease (tr dec): Holding back last lp of each st, tr in each of the sts indicated, yo, pull through all lps on hook.

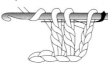

Example of 2-tr dec

Slip stitch (sl st): Insert hook in st, pull through both lps on hook.

Chain color change (ch color change) Yo with new color, draw through last lp on hook.

Double crochet color change (dc color change) Drop first color, yo with new color, draw through last 2 lps of st.

Treble crochet (tr): Yo twice, insert hook in st, yo, pull through st, [yo, pull through 2 lps] 3 times.

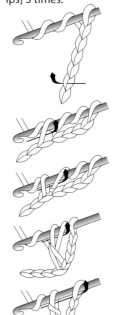